Leverage Points

A Universal Guide for Success in Dealing with Local Government

Leverage Points

A Universal Guide for Success in Dealing with Local Government

By

Richard V. Luchessi

and

Alec I. Ostrom

About the Authors

Richard V. Luchessi is a retired community college administrator and instructor with deep experience in local government. He earned his B.A. and M.A. degrees in Social Science at California State University San Jose and he also did graduate work at the Claremont University Graduate School via a General Electric Fellowship in Economics and via a U.S. State Department Fellowship in Yugoslavia. He served as the Dean of Social and Behavioral Sciences at American River Community College in Sacramento, California, and he was an instructor there in economics and history. He also served on the following (all in California): The Placer County Republican Party Central Committee, the Roseville Community Hospital Board of Directors, the Sierra City Fire Commission, the Sierra County Board of Supervisors and the Sierra County Grand Jury. He also retired as a Captain in the United States Marine Corps.

Alec I. Ostrom retired after a thirty-two year career in public high school education. He served as the Assistant Superintendent for Curriculum and Instruction with the Roseville Joint Union High School District in Roseville, California, where he also served as a school social studies teacher, vice principal, and principal. He earned his B.A. in Political Science from the University of California at Berkeley and his M.A. in Education Administration from California State University Sacramento, did graduate studies at the University of the Pacific in Stockton, CA, and was also an extended education instructor with Chapman/Brandman University. He is now the owner of Ostrom & Associates, an educational consulting firm, and has deep experience and expertise with private-public partnerships, organizational management and transformation, and Applied Systems Thinking. He served on the Roseville, CA Library Commission, the Placer Credit Union Board of Directors (Auburn, CA) and was the President and Managing Partner of Learning Integrity, Inc., an educational/business consulting firm.

Why a book on how to achieve success in dealing with local government?

Most high school and college courses don't provide much in the way of current, useful and practical information about how to deal with local government. They tend to be focused on the U.S. Constitution, the federal government and state governments. Also, when we talked with a wide variety of people we found a real concern about problems and issues with local government in their communities, and a high level of frustration and dissatisfaction in their attempts to deal with local government. We saw a clear need and a strong demand for a practical, effective set of methods, processes and "tools" which would enable all citizens and citizens' groups to deal successfully with their local governments.

Acknowledgements

This book is the product of a number of vital relationships and in-depth conversations over many years. The authors would like to acknowledge and thank the following individuals and groups in the certain knowledge that without their help and support we would not have been able to create this book.

Don Prentice: He taught us the principles and practical applications of Applied Systems Thinking and so generously provided us with some of the "tools" that will help all citizens and citizens' groups, as they achieve success in dealing with their local governments.

Dr. Hans Ostrom and Rod Collins: Helped us with the whole process of independent publishing. Dr. Hans Ostrom was also our chief editor.

The following friends, colleagues, family members and authors who provided us with their deep understandings of local government and their insights into the world of local politics-- please note that they are not listed in any particular order: Dr. Peter Drucker, Supreme Court Justice Louis D. Brandeis, General Anthony Zinni, Dr. Timothy Ferris, Ambassador George F. Kennan, V.O. Key, President Dwight D. Eisenhower, Dr. Peter Senge, Don Russell, Jim Collins, Dr. Gordon S. Wood, Dr. S. I. Hayakawa, Dr. Ron Feist, Patrick Godwin, Brian Hack, Dave Tooker, Nordis Ostrom, Dawn Brown, Sven Ostrom, Katie Palatinus, Al Pratti, Robert Tomasini, Scott O'Connor, Dr. Gottleib Baer, Dr. Robert L. Heilbroner, General Lewis B. "Chesty" Puller, Dr. Robert MacIlvenna, and Dr. Floyd Mullanix.

Introduction

Do you have political power[1]? The answer to this question may seem obvious: of course you do. If you can influence at least one other person, you have political power.

Moreover, as a United States citizen, you have the right to vote in local, state, and federal elections, the right to meet and work with other people, and the right to state your political views.

You also have political power as a consumer in the economy. If people decide to stop buying a product or service their political power is quickly felt. Back in the 1950s Ford produced the Edsel. It turned out to be a complete flop, very few people bought it, and Ford stopped producing it after only three years.

As you see, there is power in numbers. When you deal with *local government*[2] it pays to develop a group of people with a common focus and common goals. Local government officials understand clearly that when large groups of people show up at a town council meeting they, the local bureaucrats, had better pay attention.

You have political power by virtue of the people you know and communicate with regularly--your personal network. As the adage goes, it's not what you know, but whom you know.

How can you use your political power to work with local government to achieve the goals you seek?

You and your group will need to get yourselves well organized. You will need an effective team structure, solid operating processes and working relationships, a clear command hierarchy, sound businesslike fund-raising mechanisms, and carefully selected spokespersons.

Political power flows to those groups who focus on specific goals and actions. When dealing with local government you and your group need to home in on a particular issue or a limited set of goals. Such broad appeals as "we need a stronger community economy" are too general and are usually shuffled off to the town hall wastebasket. You will need to clearly define and describe *in writing* exactly what you want to accomplish, why you want to accomplish it, how you think it can be accomplished, and how it will benefit significant numbers of people in your community.

Political power flows to those who have solid information. If you want success in dealing with local government, you need to do your homework. You and your group need to become well informed on the issues you pursue and learn how the government entities that normally deal with your issue operate. You will need to get to know the key government players and how they function. You will need to become fluent in the language of local government: the nomenclature, the acronyms, and the jargon (please see the Glossary).

Political power flows to those who are well funded and who know the right people. Let's get real: money talks. Most political changes take time, energy, hard work, and solid information, and your group will need money to support and sustain these efforts. You will need to establish effective fund-raising operations. Moreover, you will need to develop productive and honest working relationships with the key players in local government.

Success in dealing with local government requires a complete and accurate understanding of the fundamentals of local government. No doctors would think of performing surgery on patients without knowledge of human anatomy and physiology. No pilots would think of flying without knowledge about the aircraft and timely information about flying conditions. Most Americans, however, are largely unaware of what really goes on in local government. They are busy working, taking care of their families, and living their lives.

Just like a professional boxer, the professional politician has been in the ring and has put in hundreds of hours sparring with his opponents. He has gotten his nose bloodied and he knows the ropes! If you are going to get in the local government "ring" with a pro, you had better know the fundamentals.

Some typical examples of citizen complaints about dealing with local government bureaucracies include: Property taxes are too high; police or fire services are too slow, are inconsistent, or too costly; garbage collection is inconsistent, poorly done or too costly; local streets and roads are poorly maintained; there is too much housing development (sprawl) or not enough housing development; there is too much crime and violence; local government officials are incompetent or corrupt; the services provided by local government are of low quality or are too costly. Complaining, however, won't get you anywhere. You need to learn the fundamentals of local government and how to influence the *leverage points* in your local government.

Any type of local government is a political *system*, (please see Glossary) established to deliver such specific services and products to the people as fire and police protection, drinking water, sewage and garbage disposal, and the maintenance of streets and roads. Each part is connected to all the other parts. To deal effectively with local government, citizens must understand these connections, how they work, and how to influence them. The decisions made in the Planning Department for example, are often influenced or limited by decisions made by the Finance Department.

Start by connecting to the right parts of your local government. This may seem obvious, but people often fail in their efforts to work with local government because they take their issues to the *wrong part of the system* (If you want to build a new home or a new business, for example, you need to start with the Planning Department and/or the Building Department).

Focus on specific *leverage points* in the system. A *leverage point-*[3] is any place in the local system where minimum efforts by citizens can get maximum responses.

Let us look at a case study involving a community's desire for better and more playground equipment. Some local citizens in a medium-sized city wanted to put in playground equipment for their children in three local city parks. They wisely decided to find out what *all* the requirements were in order to get the equipment purchased and installed.

They set up several teams and each team scheduled meetings with individuals in the departments of Planning, Police, Parks, Finance, and Personnel, as well as the city's legal counsel and the Mayor's Office. At each meeting they asked for information on what *specific requirements* would have to be met in order to get the new equipment installed, emphasizing that they did NOT have any specific proposals in mind, that they were just *seeking information for planning purposes.*

After each meeting the teams reported back to the larger citizen's group with their findings. They set up a team of three more people to record and organize the documents they received.

After three months of meetings they put together a draft for the new playground equipment and took this proposal *to another round of meetings with all the same departments and people with whom they had previously met.* Again they asked for guidance and listened carefully, documenting everything they were told, and revised their proposal accordingly. Then they invited a city council member, the mayor, and several prominent local business leaders to a meeting where they presented their proposal and asked these local power holders if they would co-sponsor the proposal when it was submitted to the city government. The local leaders agreed to do it, not just because it was so comprehensive, carefully planned and meticulously detailed, but because *these leaders had been part of the process all along the way.*

The group then delivered copies of their proposal to the same departments and people and again sought guidance to move the proposal through the correct review process. This took *three more months,* but when the proposal finally appeared on the city council agenda it was approved unanimously, and three months later the playground equipment was installed in three city parks.

What these folks did, in a very carefully planned and orchestrated manner, was to touch on all of the *correct leverage points* in their local government system. It is important to note that by doing so they encountered no setbacks, no barriers, they made few mistakes, and *wasted no time or energy having to overcome negative responses.* It took them several months of sustained work. This may *appear* to be a long time, but in the world of local government it is not.

* * * * * * * * * * * *

Any layer of local government is made up of structures known as *bureaucracies* (please see Glossary) To be successful, local citizen groups must become expert in bureaucratic ways and the people who manage them. Most types of local government are roughly structured as pyramids (please see Figure 1).

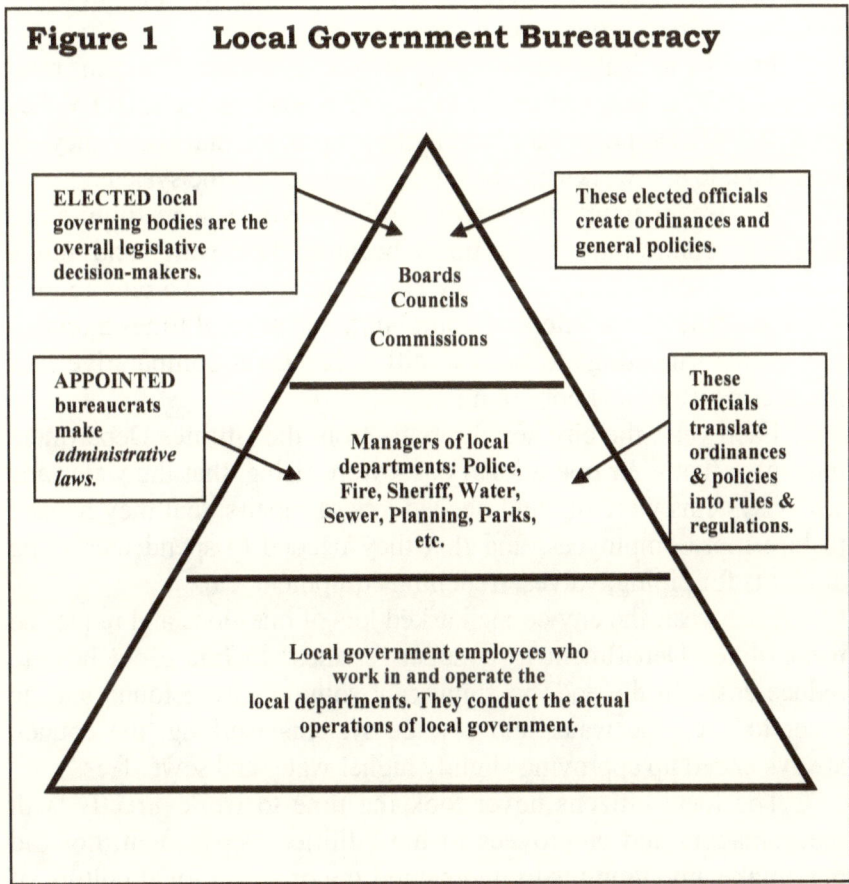

Figure 1   Local Government Bureaucracy

ELECTED local governing bodies are the overall legislative decision-makers.

These elected officials create ordinances and general policies.

Boards
Councils
Commissions

APPOINTED bureaucrats make *administrative laws.*

Managers of local departments: Police, Fire, Sheriff, Water, Sewer, Planning, Parks, etc.

These officials translate ordinances & policies into rules & regulations.

Local government employees who work in and operate the local departments. They conduct the actual operations of local government.

At the top of the pyramid is the main governing body: town or city council, county or parish board of supervisors, fire district or water district, a school board, etc., and it also includes local court systems.

The next layer of the pyramid includes the departments, and each department typically has a manager who can either be elected by the voters or appointed by the local governing body. These managers are *bureaucrats.*

The bottom layer of the pyramid includes the government employees who work in various departments, and who are also bureaucrats.

The most important thing to know about these people who work in a local bureaucracy is that they are there to accomplish the goals of the local government entities. *Their loyalty is to the local government first, and to the people second.*

In order to deal successfully with local government, citizens must learn WHO the bureaucrats are *by name*, WHAT they do, HOW they do it, WHO their bosses are (whom they report to), and HOW they are connected to and work with the other bureaucrats in the system.

A case in point: the citizens of Sunnydale, a medium-sized suburban community, were upset because their water and sewer rates kept rising each year. They called the mayor, the city council members, they sent letters of complaint, and several times attended city council meetings to protest, citing far lower comparative fees in other nearby local communities.

Each year, the city heard reports from the Utilities Department managers that their operational costs were rising, that the water and sewer systems were old and needed lots of repairs, that they needed to hire more employees, and that they needed to spend increasing amounts for piping, valves, trenching equipment, etc.

Each year, the city council asked lots of questions and requested the Utilities Department to conduct "studies" to figure out how to reduce costs. In the end, no significant solutions were found and, in order to keep the water and sewage systems working, the council always ended up approving slightly higher water and sewer fees.

The local citizens never took the time to work directly with the managers and employees in the Utilities Department, nor did they make any attempts to understand the organizational culture of the department. They never found out that the local city ordinances under which the Utilities Department operated were outdated and inefficient. They remained angry and frustrated with their local government and had high levels of distrust trying to work with the city council, the mayor, and the Utilities Department manager and employees. Ironically, these citizens kept re-electing the same people to the city council because in other areas of local government they felt that they were doing a reasonably good job.

What is wrong with this picture? Where did the citizens go wrong?

The citizens of Sunnydale did not have the right information about the local government bureaucracy, or how it really functioned, what the relationships really were, or any knowledge of the legal and cultural restrictions under which these bureaucrats operated.

Also, the citizens of Sunnydale did not use *leverage points*. They were amateur politicians who were defeated by the insider pros who believed that they, as city government bureaucrats, were just doing what they were supposed to do.

* * * * * * * * *

What then is political power? *It is the ability of a person or group of people to influence the actions of others.* This definition raises some important questions that must be considered as we work to achieve the "insider" knowledge critical for success in dealing with local government.

When we look at any level of local government we find that those who have the power keep it, use it, and expand it by controlling the flow of information to those who have less political power. If a person does not know something he or she cannot act on it.

Working with local government comes down to a very important personal choice: you can choose mostly to ignore government, to remain largely ignorant of how it really works, and hope to avoid any interactions with government. Or you can choose to be well-informed about local government and to get involved at some level that is workable and effective.

This book will provide you with the "insider" strategies, processes (leverage points), tools and techniques you need to deal effectively and successfully with local government.

Table of Contents

Chapter 1

Pragmatism:
A Strategy for Dealing Effectively
with Local Government

The formal structure of local government in all fifty states is a *charter*[1] that includes a *system* of governance processes, rules, and regulations. When we cut through all of the verbiage of these *charters* and look at local government from a *pragmatic perspective* we see that local government is a *necessity* and the people who govern (elected officials, managers, and employees) are there to implement local government processes, rules, and regulations. When local citizens petition local government to do something, they need to follow a guiding strategy of *pragmatism.*

The guiding strategy of *pragmatism* is built around some simple, direct, and sometimes counter-intuitive principles that we like to call "the rules." In playing childhood games or participating in organized activities in our schools or communities we all had to learn "the rules." Local government is not a game, but it does have its rules; some are written and some are unwritten.

Let's begin with the written rules. Most Americans already know these rules but we will quickly summarize them as follows: All American citizens, once they reach age eighteen, register to vote, and establish a legal residence in a given community or location have the following rights in dealing with local government:

- The right to vote on local issues and to elect local government officials.

- The right to form groups to work together to influence local government.

- The right to petition local governments and to require local government officials to respond to questions or complaints.

- The right to sue local governments or to take other legal actions against local government.

- The right, in most states but not all, to recall elected officials and to hold an election to remove them from office.

- The right to have local government meetings that are open to the public and the right to speak to local government officials at those meetings.

The strategy of *pragmatism* in dealing with local government is all about local citizens learning HOW to most effectively use both the written rules AND the unwritten rules to get local government to do what they want it to do.

The "insiders" know all about the unwritten rules, ("rules" created over time as reflections of local traditions, customs, and local political cultures) and here they are:

1. **As much as you possibly can, remove your egos, interests, and personalities from your strategy, your plans, and your actions in dealing with local government.**

   All human beings have egos, interests, and personalities, including local government officials, managers, and employees (bureaucrats), and so do local citizens who are petitioning their local government to take action on some issue. Success in dealing with local government is all about keeping your focus on your *purpose* and your *desired outcomes* and not allowing individual egos or personal interests to get in the way.

   When citizens allow their egos, interests, and personalities to have too much influence on what they are doing, they often go to City Council or Board of Supervisors meetings and insult the government officials, berate them, "demand" things, and/or deliver emotional ego-centered speeches that criticize or belittle local government officials or employees. The result is that government officials usually just write them off—either by ignoring them or by burying them in complex bureaucratic procedures and endless detail.

2. **When dealing with local government officials, managers, and/or bureaucrats take the time to get to know them as individuals and as people who perform certain roles in local government.**

    This may seem like a direct contradiction of what we just stated in rule #1 above, but it really isn't. All local government officials--be they council members, county or parish supervisors, judges, department managers, or government employees (bureaucrats)--have official roles to play and, at the same time, they are all just people: individual human beings with egos, interests, and personalities.

    To have success in dealing with local government, you and your group will need to establish *professional working relationships* with local government officials and employees. This means that you need to find out what their individual roles and responsibilities are *and* how they typically do their work to fulfill their official duties.

    It also means getting to know them as people. What kinds of things catch their interest? What are they really passionate about? What sorts of things turn them off or cause them to react negatively or irrationally? Are there specific words or descriptions that trigger angry reactions or cause them to stop listening? It is equally important for local citizens to ask these same questions of themselves to prevent emotional, angry, or unplanned responses to the people in local government.

3. **Listen to what local government officials, managers or employees (bureaucrats) are saying—the content and the facts—and reserve judgment until the last words are spoken.**

    Take the time for *direct conversations* with the people in local government. Talk informally with government officials, managers, and employees (bureaucrats) before meetings, after meetings, and in other informal settings. Ask questions that are neutral (not loaded) and questions that seek information. Ask for their guidance and advice and take advantage of their expertise.

Read and study what they have written or presentations they have made. Check out their websites and press clippings and talk to people who may know them well. And above all, *listen to them* and *read their body language.* When they are talking during a meeting or when they are working with you, *listen carefully* to what they are saying, *to what they are NOT saying* and *to what their body language is saying.*

Finally, please do not berate them, insult them, criticize them or verbally attack them. It is okay to disagree with them or question them, but do so in a respectful, professional manner. And if government officials, managers or employees start berating you, *remain silent and do not get into confrontations with them.* Always remember: *Do not feed the irrational monkeys; it just makes them worse.*

A brief comment about BUREAUCRATS: Americans often hear and see the term "bureaucrat" used as a negative word to describe a government official, manager or employee and the working assumption is that these people are uncaring, lazy, stupid, rude, arrogant, and generally unresponsive to local citizens. In 99% of the cases, this working assumption is simply UNTRUE. Bureaucrats are usually managers or employees who work for some department, agency or bureau of local government. Most of them are well trained and most of the time they do their jobs in a caring, engaging, effective and positive manner. Please take the time to get to know them and please do NOT assume that they are bad people or somehow corrupt, uncaring, condescending or unresponsive; they aren't. They are regular people who just happen to work for the local government.

---

4. **Take the time to learn everything you can about the formal lines of government communication, decision-making, the delivery of services, and the informal and usually invisible lines of communication, behind-the-scenes relationships and behaviors.**

All types of local government are *political systems* and they are also *bureaucracies.* Political systems and bureaucracies are specialized kinds of organizations and they have unique organizational "cultures" or ways of doing things. We have prepared two diagrams for you to illustrate these two different but related perspectives of *any type* of local government. Please carefully review Figure 2 and Figure 3 below.

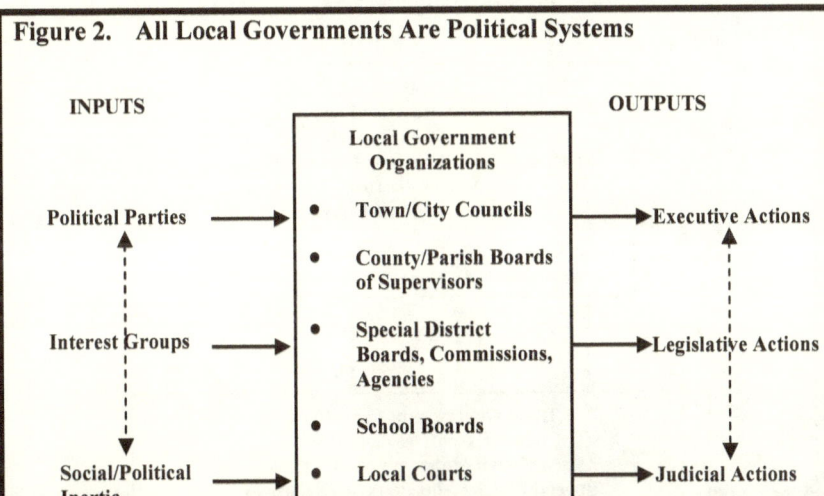

Figure 2.   All Local Governments Are Political Systems

The Economic, Social and Physical Base

All local governments exist within the context of the local or regional economy, society/community and within the physical realities of a local or regional geographic area: rivers, streams, mountains, farms, factories, minerals, trees, swamps, harbors, ocean front, coast lines, lakes, etc.

INPUTS = People, groups, organizations and forces that influence local government decisions and actions:

    Political Parties in some states choose some local candidates, run political campaigns, and get certain local government officials elected.

    Interest Groups are well-organized groups of people, associations, unions, etc. who provide specialized information to local government officials, usually through professional representatives or lobbyists.

    Social/Political Inertia is the weight and force of local/regional traditions, customs and values. It is "how we do things around here." It is a force for doing things the way we have always done them. It is often unseen but it is very powerful.

OUTPUTS = Actions taken by local governments to conduct business or to deliver government services or programs:

    Executive Actions include administrative rulings, management decisions, and day-to-day operational decisions and actions of government departments, agencies, etc.

    Legislative Actions include the creation of policies, ordinances, general plans, etc.

    Judicial Actions include court orders, writs, and judicial decisions or rulings.

The dashed vertical arrows are the *informal lines* of communication, decision-making and working relationships.

Figure 3.   All Local Governments Are Bureaucracies

Solid lines = formal lines of communication, decision-making & working relationships.
Dashed lines = informal lines of communication, decision-making & working relationships.

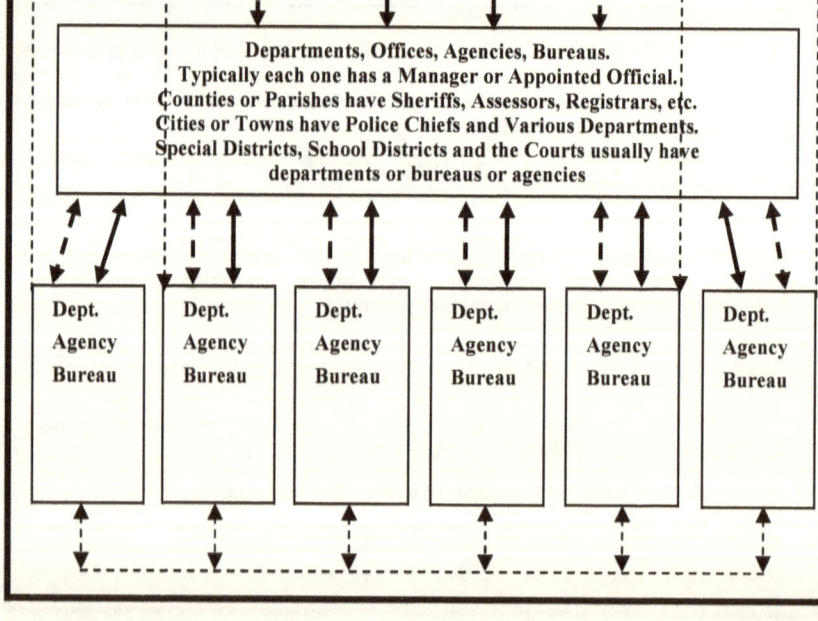

Local Government Ruling Bodies:
County or Parish Boards of Supervisors
City or Town Councils
Special District Boards or Commissions
School Boards
Local or Regional Courts

Note: In most cases, these officials are elected by the voters, but, in some cases, they are appointed.

Local Government Executives:
County Executives or Managers
City or Town Managers and/or Mayors
Special District Managers or Executives
School Superintendents
Judges or Administrative Law Judges

Departments, Offices, Agencies, Bureaus.
Typically each one has a Manager or Appointed Official.
Counties or Parishes have Sheriffs, Assessors, Registrars, etc.
Cities or Towns have Police Chiefs and Various Departments.
Special Districts, School Districts and the Courts usually have departments or bureaus or agencies

| Dept. Agency Bureau | Dept. Agency Bureau | Dept. Agency Bureau | Dept. Agency Bureau | Dept. Agency Bureau | Dept. Agency Bureau |

The more knowledge and "insider information" that you and your group can obtain about the *formal* and the *informal and often invisible* lines of communication, decision-making and working relationships both *inside* and *outside** your local government, the more effective you will be. Remember, you may just be dealing with one department to get what you need, but that department is *connected to and influenced by ALL of the other departments, officials, and bureaucrats in your local government.*

---

* Note: We will help you with the OUTSIDE influences on local government (lobbyists and interest groups) in Chapter 2 and Chapter 3.

---

5. **Speaking and understanding the language of local government ("legalese" and "bureaucratese") is critical for success in dealing with local government.**

   When you and your group attend your first City or Town Council meeting, or Board or Parish Supervisors meeting, or Special District Board or Commission meeting, you will suddenly discover that they use words, phrases and acronyms that may sound otherworldly. This is the "insider" language or nomenclature of local government and you and your group will need to learn it and use it to your advantage.

   Here are some strongly recommended resources to help you learn the "insider language" of local government:

   - Talk *informally* with local government officials and employees and ask them to help you understand what certain words, phrases, acronyms mean. For example, if you hear a reference to an EIR (which is an Environmental Impact Report), ask a manager or bureaucrat what an EIR is, what it includes, and why it is necessary.

   - Check local government websites and gather as many local government documents, reports and publications as you can.

   - Read these documents and build your own working file of "insider" words, terms, descriptors, phrases, acronyms.

Figure out what they mean and when and how they are typically used.

- We have provided a Glossary for you at the end of this book and we have also defined certain terms, words, phrases or acronyms within the text of each chapter.

You and your group will become even more knowledgeable and "expert" if you also create your own glossaries, because you will learn the government "language" that is unique to your local community or region. Remember, when you ask or petition your local government to do something, you and your group need to "speak" to them in *their language,* not yours.

6.   **Local governments operate--in fact, they thrive--on statistics-[2] and numbers. Read any and all government documents, agendas, and reports very carefully and focus on the statistics and the numbers. Take nothing for granted and do not assume that statistics or numbers are correct. Remember: The context in which statistics or numbers are used or stated means everything.**

The bottom line here is that local governments are driven by numbers and statistics, and those who have the "insider" numbers and statistics can influence local government to get many things decided in their favor. The "insider" trick here is to learn how local government officials, managers and employees *think about* numbers and statistics, and to understand how they *use* numbers and statistics to *make decisions.*

Here are some common and helpful examples your group will need to study and use to support your case for what you want your local government to do:

- Budget and financial documents and reports
- Traffic accident and traffic flow studies.
- Reports and documents on the frequency of certain crimes in your area or community.
- General plans or specific area plans for housing or commercial business developments.

- Reports and documents on local government fees and service charges.

- Reports on comparative salary and benefits studies for local government official and employees.

- Reports on health care benefits for local government officials and employees.

Never accept government statistical studies or reports at face value. Statistics are researched, prepared and written by people who have their own perspectives and biases. A "statistical fact" in and of itself means nothing; it is the *context* of where and how a given set of statistics is used that makes all the difference.

When a report says that crime rates have increased by 23% you need to ask: Increased relative to what? Last month's crime rates? Last year's crime rates? Crime rates for small towns? Crime rates for rural areas? And what are the *trends* in crime rates for the last ten years?

Here, again, it is important to build those *professional working relationships* with local government officials and employees, because they can often provide you with statistical reports or studies *that are not usually provided to the general public.*

Also, designate one or two people in your group to become the "numbers experts" who take the time to study and analyze statistical reports and documents, and who learn to "read between the lines" to figure out critical statistics that may be missing, incorrect, or biased. If you have the financial resources, hire some experts to help you figure out and analyze the statistics.

And remember, when you and your group question the "numbers" or statistics presented by government officials or employees, *you need to be fully prepared for them to question your "numbers" or statistics.*

Focusing on the numbers and the vital statistics will also help you to keep your egos, interests and personalities out of your working relationships with local government officials or employees. Numbers and statistics are impersonal, factual and concrete, and they are much harder to argue with than people who are uninformed and overly emotional or personal.

7.   **Finally, and most importantly, follow the money.**

To achieve your *purpose* and your *desired outcomes,* you will have to show where the money will come from to pay for them. Local governments, by law, must follow fairly strict budgetary guidelines and procedures. Government employees can't just wave a magic wand and hand you and your group money, just because you ask for it.

In most cases, the money is there somewhere in the coffers of local government but bear in mind that [a] you and your group will need to find it; [b] you will be competing with other departments and agencies who already have their own budgets and plans for using the money; and [c] you also will be competing with outside groups who have their own proposals or requests, and some of them may be special interest groups with professional lobbyists.

When you present your request or your proposal, one of the first questions the officials or employees will ask is, "How do you plan to pay for your proposal?" If your group does not have a solid, well-researched, airtight set of answers to the "money question," then your chances of success will be very slim.

By law, local governments must provide copies of their budgets upon request, although you may have to pay a fee for each copy. But remember: There is a budget "language," there are budget rules and there are "insider" budget maneuvers that local government managers and employees utilize. Your group will need to develop at least two individuals who become experts at the budget "language," rules and "insider" maneuvers. And one final note: much of the funding for local governments comes from the state or the federal government, and this funding *always comes with lots of additional rules and regulations.* Your group will need to become familiar with these rules and regulations as well.

That's it: Seven simple, direct, and practical "unwritten rules" for dealing successfully with local government. These "unwritten rules," and the short list of "written rules" noted above, constitute our strategy of *pragmatism* in dealing with local government. Keep it professional, stay focused on your *purposes* and *desired outcomes,* keep the egos, interests and personalities out of it, and follow the pragmatic rules we have recommended, and you and your group will be well on your way to getting your local government to do exactly what you want it to do.

"Anything is possible if you put your mind to it and you really work hard and you bring the right perspective to it. You shouldn't focus on why you can't do something, which is what most people do. You should focus on why perhaps you can, and be one of the exceptions." – Steve Case, Founder of AOL

Chapter 2

A Toolbox for Dealing Successfully with Local Government

The realistic application of the seven "unwritten rules" described in Chapter 1 requires people who seek changes or actions by local government to band together in "citizen interest groups," which are directly engaged in the politics and political processes of local government. Many Americans see politicians and the political process as something unsavory and sometimes tainted by corrupt political practices, so they have serious concerns about getting involved or engaged in local government.

People are people, and a small minority of them will always try to take "shortcuts," or they will try to fill their own wallets. This kind of corrupt behavior has been going on since human beings first emerged from their caves and formed tribes or clans (the first forms of local government). So here's another hard truth: citizens or citizens' groups who want to be successful in dealing with local government have to become *politicians** and they have to enter into the world of *local politics.*

---

* *Politician* defined: The Merriam-Webster Collegiate Dictionary, 11th Edition, identifies a *politician* as "a person experienced in the art or science of government; one actively engaged in conducting the business of government." Contrary to many negative connotations about the title *Politician* currently used in the media, we believe the Merriam-Webster definition to be the most accurate.

The two levels of local government which are the most common across all fifty states are cities and counties (parishes in Louisiana), and they will be the working context for this chapter.

In later chapters, we will get into the more specialized areas of local government, such as special districts, school districts, and local courts but, for now, we will work in the most familiar political arenas of *cities and counties.*

To illustrate how they work, we will focus on a serious issue that is common to all towns, cities and counties across America, namely, increasing problems with *crime.* No one is immune to *crime,* no matter where they live, and many people are very concerned about the effectiveness of law enforcement in their local communities. This will not be a formal case study but it will serve as our working example.

Let us imagine that you and your neighbors are upset, concerned, and maybe even angry with what appears to be an insufficient, inconsistent and ineffective level of law enforcement in your neighborhood, town, city or county. What can you do about it? Where should you begin?

Quite often, when people in a neighborhood or community get fired up about some problem or issue, one of the first things they do is to put together a loosely-structured committee of volunteers. The committee members then choose a chairperson or leader (many times by default--usually the person who is the most outspoken), start making rapid decisions on what they want to do, and then they leap into action.

What we soon discover and observe, however, is another hard truth--most of the committee members are just that, committee members. They are not really interested in doing much work and they frequently delegate the work to the leader or to other people in their neighborhood or community. They are very passionate at first but, as time goes on, they tend to get tired, bored and impatient. These ad hoc committees typically do not have the "right people on the right bus"[1] and, before too long, there is internal squabbling or people start to miss the committee meetings or show up late, and soon the whole effort begins to wobble and fall apart.

We strongly advocate that all citizens and citizens groups begin by forming an *Effective Action Team* (EAT). An EAT is a collaborative, mutually-supportive *team*; it is *not* a committee. An *Effective Action Team* is well-trained, well-practiced and disciplined. It has the following characteristics:

- An EAT has the *"right people* on the bus: solid leaders, effective spokespersons, researchers, fund-raisers, bookkeepers or accountants, secretaries, documentarians and publishers, technical support people, and day-to-day operational managers. Each person on the team has been carefully recruited for his or her unique skills, and there are clear and effective processes and working relationships that maximize those unique skills in a well-coordinated, unified manner.

- An EAT has the *"right people* on the *right bus:"*[1] The *right bus* means that the EAT is properly focused and aligned with its stated purposes, goals and objectives. A citizens' group cannot be effective if some of its members want to go in one direction and others want to go in a completely different direction. A disunited citizens' group will "crash and burn." An EAT must have a professional, disciplined, *united* approach and strategy.

Guided by the seven "unwritten rules" and using the four tools we will describe in this chapter, local citizens can form themselves into *Effective Action Teams* which will provide them with the practical capability to deal successfully with any type or level of local government.

The first critical step in forming an Effective Action Team is to carefully recruit and select a *strong leader or leaders.* Strong leaders of EATs are people who have the following qualities and characteristics:

- A rock-solid reputation and standing in the town, city or county.

- Effective facilitators, guides and communicators. They are comfortable speaking to different audiences in public meetings and in private meetings.

- Good listeners. They are patient, and they take the time to seek out and understand diverse perspectives and creative ideas. They can handle criticism and can neutralize those who are cynical or indifferent.

- Ability to work closely and effectively with a wide range of people who have different personalities and working styles.

- Ability to delegate and to build a working context and relationships that encourage other people to be effective in their designated areas of the larger EAT operation.

- The courage of their convictions. Once the EAT has made a decision on its strategy and Project Implementation Plan, they are willing and able to move forward with dedication, determination, and hard work.

- Advocates and champions. They remain calm in situations that unnerve ordinary people.[-2]

And just to be very clear about the qualities and skills of strong leaders, it is very important to note that strong Effective Action Team leaders are NOT:

- Dictators who think they know it all.

- Loud, forceful, overly-emotional people who verbally or physically push aside anyone who disagrees with them or gets in their way. These people are not leaders, they are bullies.

- People who are glib, or slick talkers who really have nothing substantive to say.

- People who have to be in control of everything and everyone; those who micromanage and who always have to have it "their way."

- People who are enthusiastic and passionate at first, but fade away when it comes to doing the hard work over many months, and working through the hard challenges and obstacles.

The second step is to build an Effective Action Team that has the right people on the team "bus." The initial team organizers need to reach out and recruit additional members who have the knowledge, skills, expertise and commitment to fill the necessary roles and functions to effectively implement the seven "unwritten rules" and the four tools.

It is hard to be disciplined enough to take the time and effort to form an Effective Action Team. Slipping quickly into a standard "committee" seems relatively easy and a good thing to do for quick action. Don't do it!! Take the time and do the hard work of recruiting the right people. Take the time to pull the right people into a closely-knit, strongly-committed *team* which is in the fight for the long haul. We will describe some of the necessary roles and responsibilities for the "right people" later in this chapter.

The third step is to engage the Effective Action Team members in an extensive *dialogue* to design the "right bus," and to decide where it is going. This third step is often overlooked or short-changed because people want to take *immediate action* and they just assume that everyone is on the same page and the group has already agreed on the direction of its course. It is critically important for the Effective Action Team to take the time to thoroughly discuss and come to an agreement on the kinds of questions listed here (using our crime case study as an example):

1. What exactly is the true problem or issue that needs to be solved? In our case study, we want to reduce the crime rate community but, in more specific terms, what does "reduce the crime rate" really mean?

2. What exactly is the best approach to solve the true problem or issue that the EAT has identified? In our case study, the best solution might be to have more consistent and effective law enforcement and crime prevention by the local police department or county sheriff's unit. But, again, in more specific terms, what does "much more consistent and effective law enforcement and crime prevention" really mean? It is very important for the EAT to formulate some sort of working or tentative picture of the ideal solution they intend to achieve, in order to successfully address the issue. An ideal solution may sound far-fetched, but is has two important purposes:

    • By working on an *ideal solution,* the EAT will avoid selling themselves short before they even begin. Many times, citizens' groups reject potential solutions to serious issues because they *assume* that such solutions are too expensive or too difficult and, as a result, very good ideas are left behind. In the beginning, the EAT needs to consider all potential ideas for an effective solution to a given issue, no matter how outlandish they may appear at first.

- By working on an *ideal solution,* the EAT will think collectively about both short-term and long-term actions to a particular issue. This is critically important. Most citizens' groups focus only on short-term, immediate actions and, even if they are successful in getting their local government to take such actions, the movement often fails because the necessary conditions and capacities for sustaining such actions are not put in place. An *ideal solution* addresses the immediate issue (in our case study, quickly reducing crime incidents) and it also establishes the proper conditions and capacities to reduce crime rates over the next decade or two decades.

3. What conditions need to be in place in order to achieve "more consistent and effective law enforcement and crime prevention?" This desired outcome is not going to happen by magic. It will take significant changes in several conditions: funding, time, training, informed citizens, equipment, patrol cars, perhaps more police officers or sheriff's deputies, or a bigger jail facility--the list goes on. These are examples of some of the conditions that must be in place for citizens' groups to be successful in addressing an issue, whether it is crime or something else entirely.

Experience shows that most citizens or citizens' groups (usually rapidly-formed committees or neighborhood groups) do not take nearly enough time on the *front end* of the problem or issue (in this case study, *crime reduction*) and they often leap into action with some half-baked ideas. They might bombard local government officials at city council meetings or county boards of supervisors' meetings with many heated comments but, in most instances, nothing substantive really happens.

By taking the time to thoroughly discuss these three critical questions, the members of the Effective Action Team will create a "working solution" and they will come together to agree on their common direction in working with local government. They will have a solid working "map" and the right people on the right bus, as they embark on their journey through the sometimes hostile territory of local government.

Along with the right people on the right bus with a solid vision of an "ideal solution" here are two "tools" that will help your group come together, to avoid the ineffective practices of committees, and to be much more successful in getting your local government to do what you want it to do.

The first tool is called *The Conditions for Change*™*3* and it will enable your group to do a quick but accurate and effective analysis of where you stand in trying to solve a problem or issue you have identified in your town, city or county.

Any proposed new solution (such as more consistent and effective law enforcement and crime prevention) to an identified problem or issue (growing crime rates) involves *change*. Talking about change is one thing--actually *doing it* is much harder. In almost all situations with local government, it is the *people* in the local government who determine the success or failure of a *proposed solution* (such as more officers in patrol cars) *because it involves changes in the perspectives, attitudes, working relationships of local government officials, managers and employees and in how they do their jobs.*

The fourth step in our process is this: *Before* you and your group have any interactions with people in local government, take the time to use the *Conditions for Change* analysis tool to see if the proper *conditions* to support your desired outcomes are in place. If the proper conditions are not in place, you will quickly know what your EAT is up against, and what you will need to do. Please review *The Conditions for Change* information on the next page carefully and *use it!!*

The Conditions for Change™

The people (local government officials, managers, and employees AND local citizens) involved in any proposed change must:

UNDERSTAND THE PROPOSED CHANGE

People must understand the purpose, rationale, benefits, and implications of any proposed change. People must be fully informed participants in the proposed change process.

HAVE ADEQUATE AND PROPER RESOURCES

Necessary resources must be available: Information, time, energy, funding, expertise, training, equipment, policies, etc.

SEE THE CHANGE AS IN THEIR OWN SELF-INTEREST

People must see the proposed change as in their own self interest, as *they* see that interest. Threats of negative consequences may achieve the appearance of compliance, but they will not obtain commitment and energy.

COLLABORATE TO CO-CREATE THE PROPOSED CHANGE

If people are affected by a proposed change, they must be involved in co-creating that change. Imposing change on the people who are passive agents, or forcing change using political power is a proven formula for generating resistance and, in most cases, ultimate failure.

When all four *Conditions of Change*™ are present they will generate:

STRONG PEOPLE COMMITMENT

AND

STRONG MOBILIZED PEOPLE ENERGY

Without these *Conditions for Change*™ you will get pro forma compliance at best, and usually resistance and even sabotage.

The first two *Conditions for Change*--**Understand the Proposed Change** and **Have Adequate and Proper Resources--**

are usually understood as "common sense." Often, however, citizens' groups *assume* that these two conditions are in place when, in fact, they are not. An Effective Action Team will take the time *to examine such assumptions* by asking lots of questions of themselves and exploring a deep dialogue process to get everything out on the table where everyone can see exactly what is going on. *Everyone* in an Effective Action Team needs to be fully informed, and they need to fully understand what the proposed solution (for example, new law enforcement and crime prevention processes) is really all about, as well as the *purpose, rationale, benefits, and implications* of any proposed solution.

The second pair of *Conditions for Change*--**See the Change as in Their Own Self Interest** and **Collaborate to Co-Create the Proposed Change**--is usually much harder to perceive, understand and establish.

In our case study, for example, we ask this question: who would not be in favor of "more consistent and effective law enforcement and crime prevention" as a proposed solution? As the Effective Action Team digs into the research on increasing crime rates and *why* the crime rates have been increasing, they may discover that some people in the community would like more effective law enforcement and crime prevention but they *don't want to pay for it!* These folks may envision the distinct potential for higher property taxes or user fees, and such increased costs are not in their self interest, *as they see it.*

Here is another sample question: who would not be interested in *collaborating and co-creating* new law enforcement and crime prevention programs? Here again the Effective Action Team may discover that the police department or the sheriff's department believes that its existing law enforcement programs and crime prevention programs are working just fine, *given the available manpower and resources that they currently have.* They do not want to be seen as the cause of higher property taxes or user fees.

Many citizens in a town or city or county may *say* that they would love to work together to co-create more effective law enforcement and crime prevention *but, when it comes to actually taking the time and doing the work of collaboration and co-creation, they are nowhere to be found.* These folks are just "too busy" or they "can't find a babysitter," or "they have to take care of grandma," or any one of a thousand excuses for not doing the hard work of collaboration and co-creation.

By using the *Conditions for Change* analysis tool at the start of the process, an Effective Action Team can quickly determine if or how all four of the *Conditions for Change* can be in place (they usually aren't). An Effective Action Team will also know that if it cannot get these four *Conditions for Change* in place in a reasonable, practical, and workable manner, then the team may want to take another approach to solving the identified problem or issue *before* the members invest their time, money, and hard work.

Another "tool" that is very helpful in working out the details and conditions for a proposed solution to an identified problem is the *Fish Bone Diagram*[4]:

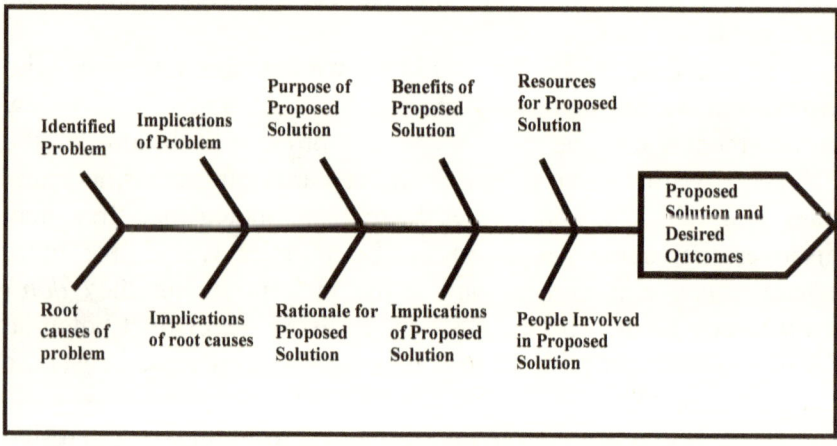

The Fish Bone Diagram can be used in different working contexts and at different stages of the problem-solving process. To clarify the first two *Conditions for Change,* it is often very helpful for Effective Action Team members to have a full dialogue about the components listed in the Fish Bone Diagram.

Let's assume for the purposes of our case study that your Effective Action Team has completed the *Conditions for Change* analysis and the Fish Bone Diagram review. The group found that *three* of the needed conditions are solidly in place and achieving the fourth seems to be within reach. In other words, the odds of success are reasonable and it is okay to proceed and to pursue the achievement of the "ideal solution." Remember: an ideal solution is not unrealistic or impractical, but the opposite. An ideal solution quickly and effectively addresses a problem or issue in the short term, and it also creates the conditions and capacities for long-term sustained implementation over five or ten years.

The fifth step in the process is to develop a ***Project Implementation Plan***[5]. The EAT needs to know exactly where it is going, how it is going to get there and how it will be able to measure the results of its "working solution" for reducing crime.

To help you accomplish step five, we have another very helpful tool we call a *Transformation Map*[6]. At this juncture we will quote briefly from the document in the Appendix for purposes of a brief illustration and explanation:

Before starting on any project to address or resolve a serious, substantive and/or complex problem or issue, it is always best to first construct a Transformation Map™ to pre-plan your action project. Leaping into action always feels good at first but without a Transformation Map™ initial enthusiasms and hard work often dissolve into frustration and failure because unforeseen obstacles emerge and there is no plan or resources to address them.

*Failing to plan is planning to fail and it is not what you think of that destroys an action project but what you **don't** think of. Taking the time to complete the Transformation Map™ pre-planning process on the front end of any action project will produce significantly greater chances for success.*

What is a Transformation Map?

Any sort of change is a transformation. A process of any kind is the transformation of a certain input into a new output. Whether we are changing something simple—such as the clothes we are wearing--or something complex, such as a law or government policy, we must engage in a process of transformation.

A Transformation Map is a "map" that guides us through any change process. In the context of our case study, the Effective Action Team needs to describe what will be included in building the "right bus" for crime reduction as well as the road map which will guide the bus to its intended destination.

Without a Transformation Map and a solid Project Implementation Plan, your EAT most likely will run into all sorts of unforeseen problems, which will make your work much more difficult and time-consuming, and greatly reduce your effectiveness and success. **Remember unwritten rule #7:** To achieve success in getting your local government to implement your ideal solution, you need to convince local government officials, managers, and employees to change the budget allocations they have already made and you will be competing with other interest groups. Without a solid Project Implementation Plan, your odds of success are very slim indeed.

On the next page, we have included a sample form which will help your Effective Action Team to develop its Project Implementation Plan. You will find that it can be expanded and adapted to fit whatever issues your EAT may be working on with your local government. This form is also listed in the Appendix.

Project Implementation Plan (PIP) Simplified Form: | Page__of__ |

Project Title: _____ **Draft #** _____ **Date:**_____

Identify and describe the problem to be solved or the issue to be resolved:
1.
2.
3.
4.

Describe the details of the Desired Outcomes that will make up the Optimum solution or resolution:
1.
2.
3.
4.

Necessary Conditions or Revised Existing Conditions to achieve the Desired Outcomes:
1.
2.
3.
4.

Action Set Number _____ **to put the Necessary and/or Revised Existing Conditions in place and the tasks related thereto:**

Action Steps:
1.
2.
3.
4.

Tasks	Dependencies	Resources	Metrics	Persons Responsible	Deadlines
1. Describe required work	Order of tasks	Time, funds, Information, Training, Equipment, Software, Expertise, Processes Etc.	How progress will be assessed in stages or phases and evaluated at project end	List names	List dates

2. Describe each task completely including processes, actions, specific work, working relationships, etc.
3. Don't assume anything; describe what needs to be done even if it seems obvious.
4. The initial tasks must put the necessary conditions in place to achieve other tasks and to achieve the desired outcomes.

There are other resources out there on how to build Project Implementation Plans, but we would urge you to start with a fairly simple plan that has all of the critical components, and then adjust it as you go.

Any workable, practical, and useful Project Implementation Plan should include the following basic components:

1. **A statement of the problem to be solved or issue to be resolved and a list of the details that are involved.** For example, when we use our increasing crime rate problem, we need to do some research and describe exactly what is involved in the "increasing crime rate." Is it more murders, more robberies or more carjackings? Or is it increases in new areas of crime such as identify theft?

2. **A statement of the *Desired Outcomes* in the Working Ideal Solution that the group wants to see in place when the problem is solved.** Here, again, you should describe each Desired Outcome in detail and in specific ways that can be *measured.* When the Desired Outcomes are achieved, how will you know that they are fully in place and working well? Also, the total collection of Desired Outcomes should comprise what your group considers its Working Ideal Solution, i.e., a solution that solves the problem immediately (lower crime rates right away) as well as a solution that provides long-term effectiveness (lower crime rates for the next five or ten years).

3. **A listing of the *Necessary Conditions* which must be established in order to achieve *each* Desired Outcome, and a list of any *existing conditions* which need to be revised or improved to accomplish *each* Desired Outcome.** A condition can include anything needed for success: time, money, people, training, equipment, facilities, information, technical systems, a strong consensus agreement for moving forward, new policies or regulations, etc. Please see the *Transformation Map*™ document in the Appendix for a more detailed explanation of *conditions.*

4. **A description of the "action sets" (tasks and steps) that must be completed in order to establish the appropriate processes and working relationships for achieving the group's goals.**

5.   **A schedule of tasks, in the proper order, with the proper resources and step-by-step measurements, identifying the "persons responsible" and clear performance timelines and deadlines.**

Yes, doing the analysis and pre-planning work and then building a solid, workable and practical Project Implementation Plan is time-consuming and it takes consistent, disciplined hard work by everyone in an Effective Action Team. It may even feel like no one is taking any ACTION to get the problem solved!!

Please be patient. Rest assured that taking quick action without a solid *Project Implementation Plan* may feel good at first, but it is a recipe for failure in most cases. And check this out: **For every hour your EAT spends on building a robust Project Implementation Plan on the "front end" of your work with local government, you will save a whole day on the "back end," when you actually implement your plans.**

The members of the city council or the county board of supervisors, and all the local government departments already have their plans, processes and working relationships in place. They know where they are going and how they are going to get there, and they have spent a lot of time, energy and hard work in putting their processes in place. Your job is to convince them to change what they are doing to recognize and address your problem and to implement your ideal solution and, 99% of the time, it won't happen without all of the preliminary planning work we have discussed so far.

Now that your citizens' group is an Effective Action Team and you have a good leader (or leaders) in place, **the sixth step** is to recruit the other key people you will need on your team, such as:

- Fund-raisers, who know how to get in-kind contributions or money from other sources. Money will be needed to pay for many of the things and having enough funds in place is critical.

- A bookkeeper and/or accountant, who will set up a working budget and keep track of your funds and how they are expended. Solid record-keeping is a must. Many citizens' groups or committees get people to contribute money to their cause in the beginning, but if they fail to have a well-documented accounting of how the money is used, this makes future contributors very suspicious and cautious.

- Researchers who know how to locate the information you will need to support your descriptions of the problem (increasing crime rates) and your preferred solution (more officers and more patrol cars) supported by lots of facts, figures and solid examples.

- Writers who will prepare all of your planning documents and research and prepare reports.

- A computer technician who will help you set up a computer network for your group and any technical equipment you may need.

- Public relations spokespersons and marketing people who will get your messages out.

- Liaison people who will work directly with government officials or bureaucrats; people who are good at building professional working relationships.

- Support staff members who do the day-to-day operations, answer phones and e-mails, do the filing, set up for events, coordinate supplies, refreshments, transportation, etc.

Please note that the key people listed above will be needed by almost all Effective Action Teams, especially if your group is dealing with a complex issue such as crime reduction and prevention. In many cases, one person may fill several of these roles, but it is usually better if your group can recruit more members to help out over time.

Assuming that your EAT has its leaders and key people in place, what are the next steps in the process of dealing effectively with local government?

Step seven is to get a detailed description of the problem (increasing crime rates in your town, city or county) that is based on solid research with well-documented and credible sources of information. Also, in developing a detailed description of the issue you will now have your first opportunity to make the *connections* you need to make with the key people in your local government. We refer to these key people as the "gatekeepers" because they can connect you to the right information, the right *sources* of information and to the *right people* in your city or county government who can guide you through the process.

Our case study of increasing crime rates will probably be familiar because many of you have most likely experienced it first-hand. But your group will need to go beyond your personal experiences to build a stronger general picture with documented evidence of the problem of increasing crime rates. So where should you begin?

Since we are dealing with a case study on increasing crime rates, an excellent start (**step 7 A**) would be to seek out some of the key people in your police department or sheriff's office. Send one or two EAT members into the police department or sheriff's office to contact someone there who deals with the general public (usually this will be a person at the front counter). Briefly describe your concerns and ask that person to help you by pointing you to the right people who deal with information concerning local crime rates. Let him or her know that, at this point, you have no specific complaints but are just seeking help and information.

Step 7 B: Next, ask the initial contact people and/or the people to whom you are referred for some general information about how the police department or sheriff's office is organized. Try to obtain as much written information as you can: brochures, handouts, flyers, public relations information, etc. Visit the police or sheriff's website if they have one and check out all of the information and resources you can find there. Visit the local public library and ask people there to help you find information about the local law enforcement agencies from books, magazines, newspaper articles, etc.

Step 7 C: If you can't meet with certain resource people right away, take the time to set up an appointment to meet with them. Let them know that your group is very concerned about *helping them* to get the resources they need to do an *even better job* (no criticisms, just help) of law enforcement and crime prevention. During your conversation, ask them what they would do if they had a magic wand and no limitations on budgets or manpower.

They may be reluctant to say anything that is too speculative or "ideal" at first and, if this happens, then ask more specific questions like:

- Would it help if you could hire one or two more officers?

- If you could purchase one or two new patrol cars or motorcycles, would that help?

- Would it help to hire one or two new dispatchers?

- Hiring one or two more undercover officers?

- If you could put an officer on campus at each high school or middle school to educate and counsel the students, would that help?

- Is there any benefit if more citizens would do a better job of securing their homes and businesses?

- In your view [Mister police officer or Madame sheriff's officer], what are the most serious crimes that are happening in our town, city or county, and what do we need to do to reduce or eliminate them?

- To really improve overall law enforcement and crime prevention programs, what would it take? More money? More manpower? Changes in local ordinances? More training for your patrolmen and detectives?

- What are some "invisible" things that most people in the public really don't see or understand that would really make a difference in how you do your jobs?

Please note: It is very important to plan and construct your list of questions well in advance for a meeting with a specific local government official, manager or employee. The *Transformation Map* process and the development of your group's Project Implementation Plan will help you with brainstorming lists of questions for which you need answers to set up the proper conditions for your ideal solution set.

Step 7 D: We have included a *sample interview form* and a *sample form for recording documented information* in the Appendix. When you meet with the "crime rates" people in the police department or sheriff's office, for example, ask them how they document crimes, how they report on the crimes that occur, and any trends on crime rates each year. Do they have an annual report? Do they have any other kinds of documents that they can give you? Do they have any public information documents on existing programs to reduce crime? Do they have a Neighborhood Watch Program? Are they doing anything to work with the children or teenagers in the public schools? Do they have a citizens' advisory group?

Step 7 E: Most of the time, the officials in the police department or sheriff's office will be helpful and they will guide your group's liaison representative(s) to a number of valuable sources of information. As you gather this information, you will need to have people in your citizen's group who read it, analyze it, and put it into some sort of well-organized filing and reference system, so anyone in your group can access it easily. If you have some talented computer people, have them organize a database to organize the information and your analyses of the information. Also, use big pieces of poster paper to create organizational charts to post on walls, so you can lay out a picture of the key people you have contacted and how they are connected to other key people in the government.

Step 8 A: Once you have enough factual information to do a pretty complete job of defining what the *increasing crime rates* problem really entails, then you are ready to start working on designing your preferred solution set (much more effective law enforcement and crime prevention).

By completing a Transformation Map, everyone in your EAT will realize that there are several different conditions that will have to be put in place in order to achieve or accomplish the desired outcomes in your ideal solution set.

Step 8 B: Another cycle of contacts and meetings with the right "gatekeepers" in the police department or sheriff's department. Ask them what *they would recommend* to improve the effectiveness of their law enforcement operations and their crime prevention operations. What you will really be doing here is filling in the details of the Conditions for Change and the Fishbone Diagram.

Who are the proper "gatekeepers" to interview and how can you identify them? The people in powerful leadership or managerial positions are usually the gatekeepers. In the case of the police or sheriff's department, this most likely would include the Chief of Police or the County Sheriff, the Patrol Captains, the captains or lieutenants in charge of the office operations and the jail, and the managers who take care of the budgets, purchasing, research, crime reporting, etc. Also, there may be a Citizens Advisory Group to contact for valuable information.

Be sure to keep the conversations about "seeking information" and "wanting to help." Make it clear that you are not there to criticize anyone or to complain. Remember, these gatekeepers are busy people. Be very conscious of their time. Arrive for appointments on time and leave on time. If they have to interrupt the meeting, be gracious, thank them, and tell them you will try to meet with them at another time when they are not so busy.

Be cordial, respectful and polite. If they say something that is critical, challenging or rude, just listen carefully, stay calm and do not respond with anger or defensiveness. Always jot down notes, and do not use a recording device--most government officials do NOT like recorders. Ask them for their business cards or, if they do not have one, ask them for the best ways to contact them by phone and e-mail. Always send a follow-up thank-you note and/or e-mail.

Step 8 C: After each meeting with these "gatekeepers" take the time to organize and re-write your notes and get your notes and any handouts or documents they give you to your analysis team members so the documents can be reviewed, analyzed and properly filed for future access. Also, carefully put each "gatekeepers" name on your big wall chart and show how each new "gatekeeper" you interview is *connected to* the other "gatekeepers" you have already interviewed. *Remember, you are building a professional knowledge base not only for the particular problem you are working on now, but for work on future problems and solutions as well.*

Step 8 D: After each meeting or any actions taken by group members, take the time to do an After Action Critique session. Sit down with the people involved in the meetings or other activities and with the leader(s) and other key people in your EAT and debrief. Ask yourselves the following questions:

- What did we learn from today's activity?

- What further information do we need to obtain or clarify?

- What kinds of things were not said? Were there some areas where the bureaucrat seemed reluctant to say anything, or cautious about what he or she was saying?

- What was our overall impression of the meeting? Did it go well, overall? Were there any difficulties?

- Did we make some good connections, and did we build a workable professional relationship with the people that we met with?

- What do we need to do better next time? How can we be better prepared in advance?

Taking the time to do an *After Action Critique* session while everything is fresh in your minds will really help your EAT to continually improve its effectiveness and working relationships with local officials your government. Be sure to jot down notes of what you learn during your After Action Critique session, and keep them properly organized so they are easy to access for future steps in your *Project Implementation Plan.*

The information from the gatekeepers in a police or sheriff's department will almost inevitably provide you with information on other gatekeepers in your local town, city or county. For example, if they mention the need for more funding to buy new patrol cars, or to hire more patrol officers, that may lead you to the Finance Department (money issues) and the Personnel or Human Resources Department (recruiting, interviewing, hiring, background checks, etc.), the Planning Department (if we are talking about a bigger jail or bigger offices or a bigger motor pool garage), and, most likely, the Mayor's office, City Manager or County Manager's office (they make or break the big decisions).

Step 9: Your EAT liaison people will need to repeat the same cycle of meetings and interviews with all of these key gatekeepers to seek information, ideas and input from them on requirements for improving law enforcement and crime prevention. Remember, all of this front end research and hard work has several important purposes:

- You are identifying the gatekeepers, and building professional working relationships with them. Hopefully, after several meetings, they will begin to trust you to some degree and will confide in you even more.

- You are identifying who the key decision-makers are and how they are connected to the other key decision-makers in other departments of the town, city or county government. These connection points are called the *leverage points* in the local government organization and, once you figure out where the *leverage points* are and who the *leverage point* gatekeepers are, you will be well on your way to achieving success in working with local government.

- You are obtaining vital and critical information from the key gatekeepers *inside the system.* This is exactly the *insider's knowledge* which we mentioned in our Introduction and in Chapter 1.

- You are getting the *inside information* you need to clarify your understanding and definition of the problem (increasing crime rates) and you are getting the facts, evidence and well-documented resources to support your proposed *ideal solution set* (better law enforcement and crime prevention).

- When you have this *inside information* it will help you to clarify any unexamined assumptions or weak spots in your plan, and to modify your proposed solution set so it is more tightly-focused, effective, practical, and "do-able."

- Finally, you are building the *high-leverage key relationships* your EAT will need for sustained work and on any future issues you may choose to tackle. Also, you are identifying potential allies inside local government and any potential resisters. As the saying goes, "keep your friends close and your enemies closer."

At this point we will assume that your Effective Action Team has completed all of its front end analysis, research work and meetings with local government officials. Now your EAT is ready to put together a draft of its formal proposal to the town or city council or to the county board of supervisors.

Step 10: One of the important *insider methods* here is to write your draft proposal in the *same format* as other proposals that have been submitted to the city council or county board of supervisors in the past, or proposals that are presently going through the process.

Step 10 A: Your EAT will need to obtain copies of the meeting agendas, documents that other groups have submitted, or proposals that the departments in the city or county government have submitted, currently or in the past. We have included some *sample proposal forms* in the Appendix.

Step 10 B: As you write your draft proposal, remember to keep it focused, clearly-stated and tightly-worded. Long, rambling, unorganized proposals will almost always be rejected. Be sure to include an appendix section, where your factual documents and supporting evidence are available to the decision-makers in a well-organized, easy-to-follow package. Clearly label your draft proposal document and its appendix supporting materials as a "DRAFT" and include a publication date.

Step 10 C: Once you have your draft proposal ready to go, have your liaison people set up appointments with the key gatekeepers you have identified. Give them a copy of your draft proposal and ask them for advice and recommendations for changes or improvements. This process will provide feedback if there are problems with your proposal, or if there are any key gatekeepers who have problems or oppose it. Hopefully, if you have done your *front end* analysis and research properly, there should not be too many problems, but it is important to meet with gatekeepers before you present your draft proposal to the council or board.

Step 10 D: When you meet with the key gatekeepers to solicit input on how to improve your proposal, ask them what the specific steps are in submitting your proposal to the council or board. Most local governments provide handouts about the process and what you will need to do, but always ask the gatekeepers to help guide you through the process. This approach recruits the gatekeepers as advocates for your EAT, and it also will help you to avoid any procedural problems along the way. *Please see samples in the Appendix.*

Step 10 E: After you have gathered the advice and input suggestions from the key gatekeepers, your EAT should meet to review and modify your draft proposal. Then re-write it into final form. Take your time with this revision and preparation, making sure your proposal documents are professionally printed and packaged, so they look good and are easy to follow.

Step 11: At the same time your EAT is preparing the final proposal package, the leader(s) and presentation members will need to prepare their verbal presentation to the town or city council or county board of supervisors. Keep your oral presentation short and tightly-focused, because yours will be only one of several action items on the council or supervisors' meeting agenda. Here are some specific action steps your EAT will need to execute:

Step 11 A: Carefully orchestrate a significant group of supporters to attend the public meeting. This group might be not only from your neighborhood but from other areas of the town or city or county. Make sure your supporters are well-informed and coached, and that they know how to get to city hall or the county offices, where to park, where to sit in the meeting room and how to behave. What counts is their *presence*. The leaders in city or county governments know that when significant numbers of citizens show up to a meeting, then something important is going to be presented.

Step 11 B: Remind your supporters to be courteous and professional. They need to be fully prepared to:

- Arrive early.
- Be silent attentive listeners when other agenda items are discussed.
- Refrain from making any loud noises, catcalls or loud comments.
- Applaud after your proposal is presented and the Q and A session is ended.
- Remain seated until the meeting is over or until there is an appropriate break in the meeting agenda (having your supporters get up and walk out right after your agenda

item will be considered to be very rude and upsetting to the council members or supervisors).

- Be patient. Sometimes city council meetings or supervisors meetings are long and boring (bring books or magazines, or writing materials to take notes)
- NOT use cell phones or iPods

Step 11 C: Your EAT will need to brainstorm about potential questions which the council members or supervisors may ask about the proposal. Again, your *front end* analysis and research meetings should provide solid ideas on any areas of concern the gatekeepers may have. When the council or supervisors ask questions, keep your answers short and to the point. Emphasize data, facts and evidence which the gatekeepers have provided. Unanticipated questions may be asked. *Don't* try to fake it by making up answers on the spot. Simply ask the council member or supervisor to repeat his or her question and, if it is unclear, ask him or her to clarify. Then respond by saying that your group will need to do more investigation and research and that you will submit a written answer to his/her question(s) within five working days.

Step 11 D: In most cases, your proposal will be "heard and reviewed" at its "first reading" (your initial presentation). Then it will be referred by the town or city council or county board of supervisors to the appropriate departments for their review and recommendations. Then your proposal will be brought back on the agenda for a "second reading" at a subsequent meeting (this usually takes 15 to 30 days). Here's where all of your *front end* analysis and research meetings with the key gatekeepers will pay off. The gatekeepers have already seen your draft proposal, they have helped your group with the initial research, they have given you input and advice on your draft proposal and, most important, *they already know who you are and what your group is all about.*

Step 12: Your EAT will need to ramp up for important work between the "first reading" and the "second reading." Your team members will need to work on the following action items simultaneously:

- **12 A:** Carefully analyze the questions city council members or county supervisors asked during the "first reading" and prepare additional answers, if needed.

- **12 B**: Prepare your leader(s) and/or spokespersons and supporters for a second brief presentation that is tightly-focused on the key components of your proposal, and why they are beneficial for the whole town, city or county.

- **12 C: Respond** to any critics or opponents who may pop up after your initial proposal. Be prepared to respond to letters to the editor of your local newspaper or critical comments on your local radio or TV stations. Answers should stick to the solid facts and evidence in your proposal, and how the specifics of your proposal will benefit everyone in your town, city or county. Don't respond to any personal attacks or irrational comments. Point out where your critics are incorrect and then correct them by repeating your key proposal points very briefly. Never get angry or emotional or personal; stay cool, calm and professional.

- **12 D: Coach** your supporters for the second public meeting, where some opponents may be in the audience. Your supporters will need to arrive even earlier than before, to secure their seats. They need to remain cool, calm and professional. They should never respond to rude or hostile comments by other audience members and they should focus their attention on the council members or supervisors. Council members or supervisors respond very favorably to groups that act professionally and they do not like rude, emotional or profane audience members. If your critics want to make fools of themselves in public, please let them. Keep your focus on the decision-makers.

- **12 E:** In almost all cases, the council or board will want to hear from the gatekeepers in the relevant departments of local government, to provide additional analysis and recommendations regarding your proposal. Listen carefully to each gatekeeper's comments and be prepared to answer any questions they raise or to provide supplemental information upon request. If you have done your homework, the gatekeepers should be on your side or at least remain neutral. This is where your *front end* work and your follow up will pay off.

Step 13: While your proposal is being reviewed by the various departments and gatekeepers in the city or county government, contact the key gatekeepers and ask them if there is any additional information they need, or if there are any parts of your proposal which need to be clarified. In short, follow up, follow up, follow up. Don't be too pushy or aggressive, but let the gatekeepers know that your group will do whatever is needed to move your proposal forward.

Step 14: Now we are at the moment of truth: the "second reading" of your proposal and hopefully a favorable approval vote by the town or city council or county board of supervisors. If your EAT has a solid Project Implementation Plan and you have done your research work, meetings and follow-up well, you should get a positive outcome. But don't be surprised if your proposal is referred back to the departments for further review, or if your proposal is delayed for some set of reasons that may be beyond your control. Naturally, your group will be disappointed if you don't get the approval you seek, but you should not react negatively in public. Ask more questions if they are needed, to clarify why your proposal is being referred for more review or delayed or, if things go badly, why your proposal was denied.

* * * * * * * * * * *

By establishing an Effective Action Team, following the seven "unwritten rules," using the professional methods and approaches described in the four "tools" and the fourteen steps we provided in this chapter, you will have created the team credibility and capability for sustained work over time. In some cases, it may take months or years to obtain a favorable outcome and your EAT needs to be prepared and committed to carry out your mission and strategy over a sustained period of time. Loosely-formed "rapid action" committees almost always give up and disband if they do not get a favorable response from their initial efforts, but your EAT will have what we call the *winning edge*.

Keep in mind that you will have high leverage connections and working relationships with the key gatekeepers already in place, and the ability to improve those connections and relationships. Your EAT will have valuable and practical experience in doing the *front end* analysis and research and you will know what it is like to go through the process. This will enable you to continually improve, to build a stronger proposal and a stronger case to support it. It won't be easy (it never is) but your EAT will have the right professional approach, methods, and the *insider knowledge* needed to sustain your *winning edge* over time.

Sometimes a proposal does not get approved simply because the *timing* is wrong and this may not be anyone's fault--it just happens. Also, there may be other political forces at work in the background that have nothing directly to do with your group's proposal, and you may have to investigate and find out what is going on behind the scenes.

Finally, it just may be that your proposal isn't all that it needs to be. That's okay. Step back, re-do your *front end* analysis and research work and see if there is something else you need to include in your proposal. Perhaps you need to abandon your proposal and move on (this is hard but sometimes it must be done). Don't get hung up on "our proposal"; there are many ways to achieve the same objectives and you may need simply to take a different approach or use a alternate strategy.

Remember, most problems or issues with local government don't happen out of the blue. Problems like increasing crime rates usually develop over several years, and the solutions to these issues are not easy (if they were easy they would already be in place). Complex problems or issues require a long-term perspective and sustained work on the key leverage points and key gatekeepers in local government over months or, sometimes, years. Professionals know that the process isn't over until all of the options and potential solutions have been explored, thoroughly researched and tested. By having your Effective Action Team in place, you can build the capacity for tenacious, professional, sustained work over time. Those who persist, who never surrender, almost always come out winners.

Chapter 3

The Invisible Government:
Special Districts and Special Interests

"Structures of which we are unaware hold us prisoner."
                                        - Dr. Peter Senge, *The Fifth Discipline*

There are two significant sectors of local government which are largely invisible to most people. This is because their functions are simply not well known or understood by most citizens and not widely reported by the media. In part, this is due to the nature of their operations and, in some cases, it is due to purposeful efforts by certain groups to keep what they do largely hidden from public scrutiny.

The first invisible sector includes a category of local government generally referred to as "special districts."[1] These unique forms of local government usually provide services related to large operations and/or specialized functions or systems. Some examples here include seaports, drinking water services, agricultural or industrial water services, sewage processing, solid waste disposal and/or recycling, cemeteries, fire protection, parks and recreation, libraries, electrical services, housing, industrial development, urban renewal or redevelopment, parking, transportation, and public health. Special districts also include public school districts, which we will investigate in some depth in Chapter 4.

The second sector of invisible local government includes an element generally referred to as "special interests." Special interests are groups of people who band together to influence the decisions and actions of various levels and types of local government. Special interests include labor unions and associations or organizations which represent businesses, community groups, social groups, political groups, religious groups, etc. Special interests also include the kinds of ad hoc citizens' groups we described in Chapter 2 as Effective Action Teams.

In Chapters 1 and 2, we described the seven unwritten rules, the four tools, and the fourteen steps for Effective Action Teams to deal successfully with local government and how they should be used to influence the widely-known forms of local government: towns, cities and counties (parishes in Louisiana). In this chapter, we will investigate and uncover each of these two sectors of "invisible government" so they become more visible and better understood by local citizens and citizens' groups. Success in dealing with and influencing these two sectors of local government requires a clear understanding of their history (how they came to be), structure (how they're organized), and functions (how they operate) and, most importantly, how they impact the lives of everyday people. We will begin with special districts.

Special Districts

In each of the fifty states there are hundreds of Special Districts and there are more than 35,000 Special Districts in the United States[2]. There are a number of names which are used to describe them:

- Special Purpose Districts
- Special Purpose Entities
- Special Purpose Units
- Public Authorities
- Public Agencies
- Town Special Districts
- Commissions
- School Districts

For the purposes of this chapter, we are going to divide Special Districts into two large groups: Special Districts and School Districts. We will explore the world of Special Districts in this chapter and Chapter 4 will be devoted to School Districts.

A Brief History

Special Districts actually emerged in the United States as early as the 1820s, and some were created in the territories of the U.S. before they became states. As the population of the United States grew, and the populations of each of the fifty states increased in the early 1900s (and then tripled in the decades after World War II), the demands on local governments to deliver specific services also increased. Towns, cities, counties and state governments struggled to keep up with these increasing demands for specific services such as fire protection, drinking water, utilities such as coal, natural gas and electricity, health services, waste disposal, transportation, and so on. Because the population growth occurred unevenly, it often involved multiple government jurisdictions. Towns, cities and counties found it difficult and costly to manage specific government services that crossed into multiple local government jurisdictions.

Starting in the 1950s, Special Districts expanded because the expertise that was required to deliver certain government services became increasingly complex and sophisticated, Towns, smaller cities and rural counties had difficulty in recruiting and training the specialized personnel needed to manage and deliver certain specific services. Even large cities and heavily populated urban counties struggled to keep up with the rapid changes in technology, laws, regulations, rules, and codes, required by the states and the federal government.

Special Districts developed in response to these realities and, unlike municipal bureaucracies which provide a wide range of government services and policy-making processes, Special Districts focused on providing only one or two specialized services.

Structure and Organization

Special Districts are legally viewed as "agencies"[3] (designated legal entities authorized by state laws) of each of the fifty States. They are formed and administered at the local level to provide the citizenry with one or more specific services. Special Districts are public entities with specific powers delegated to them by each state: the power to establish and levy taxes and fees, the power to make policies and regulations which have the force of law (administrative law), and the power to enforce policies and regulations through criminal policing powers and through civil procedures (e.g., court injunctions, court mandates, civil suits).

Most Special Districts are governed by boards, commissions or authorities (governing bodies) whose members are elected by the voters. These are known as *independent Special Districts* because their governance structure is separate from any other local governments. In other cases, the members of these boards, commissions or authorities are appointed by the state governor, county boards of supervisors, city councils or mayors of the larger incorporated cities. These types of Special Districts are known as *dependent Special Districts* because they operate under the oversight of some other local government. Some Special District boards, commissions or authorities have both elected and appointed officials.

As noted above, there are many different types of Special Districts but they all govern within legally-designated "service area" boundaries (legally defined jurisdictions determined by state or federal law). Most often, the *designated service areas* cross the boundaries of several other legal jurisdictions such as towns, cities or counties, and designated service areas can range in size from a few acres to thousands of square miles. Here are some examples:

- The Metropolitan Water District in Southern California, which serves over 16 million people in more than 2,500 square miles in six counties.[4]

- The Regional Transportation Authority in Chicago, Illinois, and its semi-independent service boards (the Chicago Transit Authority, the Metra Commuter Rail Division, and the Pace Suburban Bus Division) are among the largest special districts. The RTA district consists of the entire six-county region. By the size of its revenues and expenditures, the CTA alone was the largest special district in the region in Illinois in 1992.[5]

In most states, Special Districts are authorized under state laws known as "principal acts" and, in some cases, Special Districts are created by "special acts" of the state legislatures. "Principal acts" are broad state laws that describe how Special Districts are to be formed, what governing powers they have, how they are funded and how they govern. "Special acts" are usually narrow and specific state laws which create Special Districts in response to a very specific set of local conditions and governance needs.[6]

A good example of a Special District which was created by a "special act" (actually several special acts) is the Port Authority of New York and New Jersey. On April 30, 1921, The Port of New York Authority was established to administer the common harbor interests of New York and New Jersey. The first of its kind in the western hemisphere, the organization was created under a clause of the United States Constitution permitting Compacts between states, with Congressional consent. It established as area of jurisdiction called the "Port District," a bi-state region of about 1,500 square miles centered on the Statue of Liberty. In 1972, the organization's name was changed to The Port Authority of New York and New Jersey, to more accurately identify our role as a bi-state agency.

The organizational structure of most Special Districts is usually fairly simple. There is a governing board, commission or authority, and there is an operational staff of managers and employees who carry out the work and deliver the specific services which the Special District provides to the citizenry. Special Districts have organizational structures which range from small, simple organizations to those that are large and complex. Local cemetery districts, for example, may have a three-person board and a half-dozen employees, while a Special District as large as the Port Authority of New York and New Jersey has a 12-person governing commission with six commissioners appointed by the Governor of New York and six commissioners appointed by the Governor of New Jersey. It has its own police force, a budget of $6.7 billion (in 2009) and over 7,000 employees.[6]

Functions and Operations

Special District functions and operations also range from those that are fairly simple to those that are large and complex. One way to understand the functions and operations of Special Districts is to look at their *activities, funding and governance:*

Activities

Approximately 85% of all Special Districts are *single-function* districts which provide only *one service* such as fire protection, mosquito abatement, or waste disposal. The remaining number are *multi-function* districts which provide two or more services. For example, some *municipal utility districts* provide fire protection and parks and recreation services in addition to providing utility services (natural gas, electricity, drinking water).

All Special Districts provide specific services to the citizens who reside in their *designated service area* (legal jurisdiction). Some of the more common service activities in all fifty states include:

• Fire protection • Flood control & Irrigation • Cemetery services • Insect and pest abatement • Utility services • Sewer services • Solid waste disposal/recycling	• Transportation--buses, light rail, airports, seaports, etc. • Road and street maintenance • Hospitals and clinics • Water supplies, domestic, agricultural and industrial • Museums & cultural centers	• Urban renewal • Public housing • Services for the homeless and indigent • Parking • Parks and Recreation • Libraries

There is also one very specialized and unique category of Special Districts in California known as Local Agency Formation Commissions.[7] LAFCOs are Special Districts which have the authority to conduct public hearings, investigate, and make recommendations to counties, state agencies or state departments or, in some cases, to state legislatures on the *formation* of new local government entities. Some typical examples here include the formation of new Special Districts, new school districts, or new towns or cities. LAFCOs also handle proposed changes in the existing legal jurisdictions and service area boundaries of Special Districts, school districts, towns and cities. In California, there is one LAFCO per county. In other states, the creation of new local government entities is handled through a variety of local and state government processes.

Every state has different government systems and processes to establish or adjust the "service areas" of Special District and/or the boundary lines and legal jurisdictions of other types of local government such as counties, incorporated cities, towns, etc. Here are a few examples of how some of those systems and processes are implemented:

- In the State of Georgia, adjustments to service area boundaries can be made by groups of citizens who live in these areas and who present a petition to the county probate judges. After the required public notice, which must be published in local newspapers, the probate judges convene a Grand Jury which reviews the petitions and approves or disapproves them. Grand Juries typically have at least 20 members who are citizens appointed by the Superior Court judge in each county. Boundary line changes of service areas require a two-thirds vote of approval by the Grand Jury, and then the petition is reviewed again by the probate judges and forwarded for approval to the authorities in each respective county.[8]

- In the state of Washington, the state legislature provides authority and specifies general procedures for the formation of Special Districts. The majority of special purpose district governments in Washington are formed by a resolution of the legislative authority or by a petition to the county legislative authority. Almost all formations require a formal hearing to determine the need for the district, and in some instances a feasibility study is required for projects such as diking districts, irrigation districts, and park and recreation service areas. The formation of a district generally requires an election to determine whether the majority of residents wish to form a district and pay taxes to receive the service. A few districts are formed after a hearing without an election. Some regular levies, all excess levies, and bond levies must to be authorized by voters of the district.

  The state of Washington also has Boundary Review Boards composed of citizens appointed by the governor, the county boards of supervisors and by the city councils of large cities in each county. These Boundary Review Boards have the authority to review changes in the boundaries of service areas and may also dissolve special districts if they are no longer meeting their original purposes or have become dysfunctional.[9]

- The state of Louisiana has Parishes instead of counties, and each Parish is governed by a Police Jury (or sometimes Police Commissions or Police Councils) of between three and fifteen members elected by the voters in each Parish. The Police Juries have the same functions as county boards of supervisors, city councils, special district boards or commissions. The Parish governments in Louisiana perform most of the same functions and deliver most of the services provided by special districts in other states, but some Parishes with larger populations have special districts for fire protection, water drainage, parks and recreation, etc. The Police Juries determine the boundaries of the service areas of these special districts.[10]

Funding

Special Districts generate revenue from several sources, including property taxes, special assessments and fees. Special Districts are usually funded as *Enterprise districts* or *Non-Enterprise districts.*

Enterprise Special Districts run much like business enterprises and they provide specific services and benefits to their customers. These Special Districts are funded primarily through fees that customers pay for services. The most common types of *Enterprise Special Districts* include airports, harbors, hospitals, public transit, solid waste disposal/recycling and utility districts.

Non-Enterprise Special Districts deliver services that provide general benefits to entire communities or regions. They generate their revenues from property taxes which often include special assessments for specific services. The most common types of *Non-Enterprise Special Districts* include those which provide such services as fire protection, flood control, cemetery services, road and street maintenance, parks and recreation, libraries, museums and cultural centers.

In Chapter 1, we emphasized an important "unwritten rule" in dealing successfully with local government, namely, *follow the money.* Special Districts in all fifty states control huge amounts of taxpayer dollars and public fees. California's *Enterprise Special Districts* generated over $37 billion in revenues, and the *Non-Enterprise Special Districts* generated over $11 billion in revenues for the last year such data were reported in 2007-08.[11] As is the case with all local government entities in all states, Special Districts must prepare, approve and publish an annual operating budget, and this is one of the best places for Effective Action Teams to learn about how Special Districts really operate.[12]

Governance

There are two forms of Special District governance. About two-thirds of Special Districts nationwide are *independent districts* with independently elected boards, commissions or authorities, whose directors serve for fixed terms (typically two or four years). Most of the directors are elected by the voters, but some are appointed by governors, other state elected officials, county boards of supervisors, county managers, city councils or mayors of larger cities. One third of Special Districts across the country are *dependent districts* and their boards, commissions or authorities are governed by local counties or large incorporated cities.

The directors of Special District boards, commissions or authorities act as "agents" of the state, and their governing powers and legal jurisdictions are authorized by state legislatures and governors, under state constitutions and statutes. Typically Special District boards, commissions or authorities govern by creating *policies, regulations or ordinances* which are implemented through "administrative law," and then enforced by departments or agency bureaucracies operated by managers and employees.

It is important for citizens and citizens' groups (Effective Action Teams) to note that much of what goes on with Special Districts happens quietly and with very little media coverage. Many people are not even aware that Special Districts exist in their local communities and regions. Effective Action Teams will need to dig in and do a lot of initial investigations to learn about Special

Districts in their residential areas. EAT members will need to attend the meetings of Special District boards, commissions or authorities, and to contact their department or agency managers and employees.

Effective Action Teams will need to use all of the information-gathering processes and tools we described in Chapter 2. It is important to realize that many Special Districts tend to be somewhat *closed* governing systems. Much of what they do involves specialized technical functions and operations and they are not accustomed to citizen involvement. Special District managers and employees often tend to be somewhat reticent, and they also use specialized terminology and technical nomenclature in their operations. Engaging with Special District employees will require a patient, persistent, professional approach to get to know them as people, to understand their roles and responsibilities, and to know the specialized technical "language" they use.

Special Interests

As noted in the introductory paragraphs to this chapter, the second sector of "invisible government" includes an element of local government generally referred to as "special interests." When citizens' groups (Effective Action Teams) set out to address a problem or issue in their community or region, they must realize that there are usually a good number of special interest groups ahead of them in line. In most instances, these special interest groups have been working with local governments for many years and they already have the "insider knowledge" and "leverage points" mastered.

We must note that we specifically chose to parallel our outline of Special Districts with that of special interests because they often have an almost symbiotic relationship. Special interests are involved in influencing Special Districts, have deep "insider knowledge" about the specific services delivered by Special Districts, and they know how to cater to the governing officials and employees of Special Districts. This makes it more challenging for citizens' groups (Effective Action Teams) to work with Special Districts.

A brief definition and history of "special interests"

For as long as governments have existed, special interests have been there to influence their officials, managers and employees. Such efforts to influence them are only natural. There have always been individuals and groups who have worked in various ways to "gain the favor of the king (anyone who holds a position of political power and authority)."

In Chapter 1, we provided a diagram entitled **Figure 2. All Local Governments Are Political Systems**, and in that diagram we noted that there are three types of **INPUTS** which influence local government (or any level of government), one of which was "Interest Groups."

We defined "Interest Groups" as "well-organized groups of people, associations, unions, etc. who provide specialized information to local government officials, usually through professional representatives or lobbyists."

Special interests, then, include any sort of group, union, association or organization which works to influence the policy and operational decisions made by local government officials, managers and employees. Most of these special interests are professional associations or organizations which specialize in the business of influencing local government. Here is a list of some of the most common special interests:

- *Unions - trade unions* (carpenters, plumbers, electricians, masons, etc.), transportation unions (Teamsters), *industrial unions* (steel makers, auto workers, etc.), *service employees unions* (firefighters, police, custodians, security guards, office workers, food service workers), and *management unions*.

- *Associations - business and trade associations* (the Chamber of Commerce, the National Association of Manufacturers, insurance company associations, product associations, service associations), *political associations* (political action committees, political think tanks, political issue groups), *religious associations* (groups such as Focus on the Family, the Conference of Catholic Bishops, the Association of Evangelical Lutheran Churches, the Southern Baptist Convention, the Jewish Theological Seminary), *social associations* (these include civic, fraternal and volunteer groups).

- *Organizations* - organizations are similar in structure and functions to *associations* but, in some cases, they may be a bit more formal and/or traditional. Some typical organizations include *service organizations* (Lions, Elks, Rotary International, Kiwanis, Red Cross, Salvation Army, Optimists Clubs, Daughters of the American Revolution, faith-based clubs), *charitable organizations* (the United Way, March of Dimes, Boys Town, Rockefeller Foundation, Bill and Melinda Gates Foundation, American Cancer Society), *political organizations* (Common Cause, Center for Public Integrity, Judicial Watch, the Eagle Forum, Citizens for Ethics and Responsibility in Washington, the National Civic League), *business organizations* (Women's Business Center, National Federation of Independent Business, Junior Achievement).

These and many other special interest groups are usually represented by professionals who establish long-term relationships with local government officials, managers and employees. What they do, for the most part, is *provide information* which promotes their desired outcomes as local governments make *policy* or *operational decisions.*

Let's say that the board of directors or the commissioners of a fire protection district are considering a new policy or regulation which will require commercial business owners to install certain types of fire alarm systems or to upgrade their existing fire alarm systems to meet an improved level of technology. The board or commissioners will certainly receive lots of information on this *policy decision* from the firefighters' union, the fire insurance companies (represented by their association), and the small business owners' organizations.

Let's take a second example: the board of directors or the commissioners of solid waste district are considering a new level of code enforcement regarding solid waste regulations. This is not a *policy decision* because the policies or in this case regulations are already in place. This is an *operational decision,* which will determine how the solid waste regulations will be implemented and enforced, and the decision may have a large impact on individual homeowners, renters and small businesses, as well as large commercial solid waste disposal companies. It is a safe bet that the directors or commissioners are going to receive lots of information from certain unions (representing service employees and garbage truck drivers), from business associations representing solid waste processing companies, and from business associations representing companies that manufacture solid waste processing equipment.

The important point here is this: these special interest groups are represented by professional agents (sometimes called lobbyists) who are experts on local government (with a strong focus on special districts). Lobbyists know all of the processes and working relationships inside local government when policy decisions are involved and/or when operational decisions are pending. Lobbyists have access to the decision-makers because they work full-time at establishing long-term working relationships, and the decision-makers know that these professional agents possess the most up-to-date expert knowledge and advice.

Effective Action Teams need to understand that they have competition, in many cases, with the professional agents who represent unions or associations or other organizations when it comes to special districts. EATs need to learn who these special interests may be, and who represents them. EATs also need to find out well in advance where these special interests stand on a given issue with local government. And, EATs need to form their own working relationships with these special interest groups lobbyists. The optimum case is to make them allies and, if this is not possible, at least get to know them and the particular points of view they represent.

Because special interests and their paid professional agents frequently represent businesses or organizations with large memberships, they typically have a lot of money to support their causes. They can quickly mobilize the members of the unions, associations or organizations to attend local government meetings of the boards or commissions or authorities who are the policy makers for special districts (and for county boards of supervisors or city councils or town councils). In short, they are powerful groups to be reckoned with, and Effective Action Teams need to get to know them well. In many cases, EATs may want to emulate their influence processes, working relationships and techniques.

Effective Action Teams would also be wise not to make enemies of any special interest groups or their professional agents. Special interests and lobbyists understand competing points of view, and they usually respect other groups who are also trying to provide information to influence local government decision-makers. They have been around a long time and they know how the game is played. New EATs are, by definition, are going to be amateurs at first, until they learn the ropes. Special interest groups and their professional agents understand this. Where they draw the line is when local citizens' groups attack them with verbal assaults, shouting and complaining at local government meetings or in statements to the media. Effective Action Teams need to keep their focus on local government officials, managers and employees, and they should avoid any confrontations with special interest groups unless they absolutely have no other choice.

A final word on special interests: We often see reports on TV or in other media about corruption or unethical behavior by certain special interest groups. In today's rapid-fire Internet and cable TV world, we see many examples of blatant propaganda, information distortions and, sometimes, outright lies being used by certain special interest groups. The large majority of special interests do NOT operate this way. They understand that success in dealing with local government comes from building and maintaining long-term relationships that are based on trust, and honesty and accurate exchanges of information.

Effective Action Teams that are successful in dealing with local government are special interest groups in their own right and they act as politicians in local government political processes. Individual citizens or groups who want to influence local government but reject any involvement in politics or special interests are not being realistic and, in almost all cases, their efforts will not be effective. At times, local government politics can be somewhat nasty (and even corrupt) but citizens' groups who try to "stay above it all" are not going to have much success. By using our pragmatic strategy, our seven "unwritten rules," our four tools and our fourteen steps, Effective Action Teams will gain the "insider knowledge" and build the long-term relationships with local government that are the "leverage points" for sustained success. In other words, these Effective Action Teams will become successful special interest groups who operate like the professionals.

Chapter 4

A Unique Form of Special Districts: School Districts

In Chapter 3 we explored the "invisible" government of special districts and special interests. This chapter will focus on a unique form of special districts, namely, public school districts.

Most Americans obtained their formal academic education in our K-12 public schools, so the existence and activities of school districts are fairly well known to most people. However, much of what happens with the *governance* of local public school districts is not generally well known or understood. Here, again, we are dealing with a type of local government that is shrouded in mystery and mythology because it obscures much of what actually goes on inside the governance operations of our local public school districts.

One quick example of a popular myth: Most Americans assume that their local public school districts are governed by local school boards under the traditional doctrine of "local control." As you will learn in this chapter, "local control" is a myth. Local school districts are largely governed by the state and federal government. To better understand how this large shift in the governance happened, and what it means for those who want to deal with local school districts more effectively, we will first review its history.

A brief history of public education in the United States

In the early history of our nation, public schools were usually established by business, governmental, community or church leaders in each town or city. Typically, the local public schools were literally one-room school houses, with one teacher providing educational instruction to local children and young adults. The educational focus was on civics (good citizenship), literacy (teaching children to read and write) and numeracy (teaching basic arithmetic and beginning work in mathematics). Most children were educated in these one-room schools until they reached age 12 or 13. They completed what would be regarded today as roughly grade level 7 or 8. After this fundamental level of education was achieved, the large majority of children left school and went to work on family farms or in other jobs, mostly unskilled manual labor, or skilled crafts and trades. There were very few students, usually the children of wealthy families, who went on to private preparatory schools, and then entered into a limited number of colleges and universities.

This type of local public education prevailed in the United States from the founding of the nation until the advent of the Industrial Revolution and the expansion of larger industrial companies in the late 1800s and early 1900s. At that time, the governance of these simple community-based public schools was controlled by local leaders in government, business, community or churches. Local town or city taxes were levied to support these schools, and the local leaders hired and fired the teachers, who were usually local residents with no specialized training in education. In addition, many of the local schools were sectarian in nature, and their operations were governed by various religious denominations.

The Industrial Revolution and the growth of industrial companies, railroads, steamship lines, and canals spurred the growth of the population and the expansion of settlements into the middle and western regions of the United States. As the populations of cities and towns across America grew in the late 1800s, a prominent educational leader, Horace Mann[1], advanced the new concept of a "common school education." Mann advocated for a common curriculum, professionally-trained teachers, better-equipped schoolhouses and a longer period for schooling, until a child reached age sixteen.

Several prominent industrial leaders threw their support behind the concept of public schools, because they envisioned this system as a source to provide the factory workers and other industrial workers they needed. These business leaders worked with educational leaders who designed the public schools as replicas of the factory assembly line, with students moving from class to class and grade level to grade level. These leaders also supported an expanded version of the "common curriculum" which stressed reading, writing, arithmetic and some higher mathematics, civics and United States history. Later, in the 1920s, 30s and 40s, science curriculum was added, along with training in home economics, crafts, trades, agriculture, and industrial factory work skills.

The governance of these larger and more professional public schools evolved from the small one-room schoolhouse to public school systems with several schools in each region, and from there emerged the concept of "local school districts." These school districts were governed by local "boards of trustees" or "boards of education," whose members were either appointed by local leaders in business, government, community or churches (usually from within their own ranks) or were elected by the local voters.

Over time, these local "public school boards" became the dominant model of public school governance across all fifty states. The diagram on the next page (Figure 1) illustrates the typical governance structure in most local public school districts today.

Figure 1

Organizational Structure of Most Local Public School Districts

Voters who reside within the boundaries of a local school district elect the members of a local "board of trustees" or "board of education."

Local Public School Boards
- Usually composed of an odd number of members: 3, 5, 7, 9, etc.
- Board members are elected "at large" or from designated areas within school districts.
- Board members usually serve 4-year terms in office.
- Typically, Board members must be a minimum of 18 years old, citizens of the U.S., legal residents of the school district, and they must not be convicted felons or have a serious criminal record.
- Board members hire/appoint the superintendent, assistant district level administrators, principals, other school site administrators and the teachers.

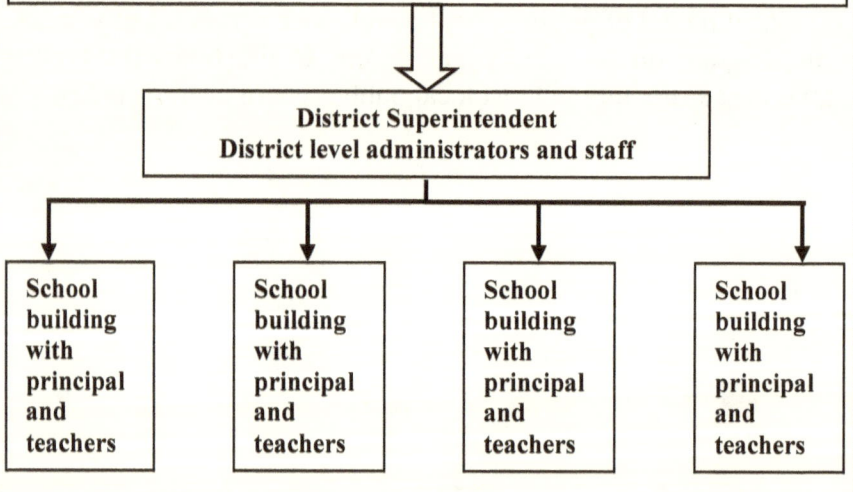

District Superintendent
District level administrators and staff

| School building with principal and teachers | School building with principal and teachers | School building with principal and teachers | School building with principal and teachers |

It is important to note that, since the 1940s, the governance of local public school districts evolved, and continues to be driven by **three fundamental and inherent** *structural conflicts*:

1. The first structural conflict emerged from the tradition of "local control" of the public schools. Even though the public school systems in all states grew to include thousands of students in local schools and districts, local leaders wanted to maintain the traditional guiding principle of "local control." This tradition of local control became more difficult to implement, however, because the majority of public school board members really didn't know much about education and learning, nor did they know how to manage large, complex, multi-million-dollar school districts. The structural conflict over local control was further exacerbated by many local members who sought election to promote their own personal agendas or to use their positions on local school boards as stepping stones to political careers at higher levels of government.

2. The second inherent structural conflict emerged because increasing numbers of parents, along with most colleges and universities, demanded that the teachers and principals in the K-12 public schools be professionally trained and certified. In the 1950s and 60s, training standards and certification criteria were raised to higher and higher levels of quality and rigor, and they have continued to be more stringent with each passing decade.

    This reality created the structural conflict between the professionally-trained certified teachers and administrators on one side, and the locally-elected school board members on the other side. A significant trend of ongoing conflicts between school board members and professional staff over curricula, teaching methods, school management, district and school finances, and other related issues grows worse with each passing year.

3. The third structural conflict was created by the expansion of the political power and authority of state governments and the federal government. All states have expanded their power and authority over public education, and so has the federal government. State and federal government leverage over local school districts has comes from their control of the *funding and regulation* of public education. In this structural conflict, local public school boards are elected by the parents and voters in local towns and cities, but the funding and regulation of local school districts is controlled by the states and the federal government. Over time, members of local school boards have become largely figureheads, with limited governing authority.

Because of these three inherent structural conflicts, the governance systems local public school districts and schools have become increasingly *closed* and *internally-referenced.*

What we mean by *closed* is that local school districts in general do *not* have any organizational channels or structures for local citizens to actively participate in school district governance through regularly-scheduled activities or meaningful processes. Local school district governance systems are set up to exclude local citizens.

What we mean by *internally-referenced* is that school district governance structures, processes and working relationships are operated and guided by internal rules and regulations and they have few, if any, connections to what is going on *outside* in local communities or regions.

Local school district administrators, at the district level and the school building level, are driven by literally thousands of federal and state laws and regulations. Over time, administrators have set up governance systems where input from parents, students and local community members is very limited, circumscribed and tightly controlled. Public school district level administrators and school building administrators generally operate with an overriding philosophy that "outsiders" (parents, students, community members, local business leaders, local government leaders) really don't understand federal and state educational laws and regulations, so there is really no need for them to be directly involved with the governance of the districts or schools in meaningful ways.

The typical involvement of "outsiders" in the governance of public schools is limited to tightly-controlled "advisory committees," "school site councils," "parents clubs," "Parent Teacher Associations [PTAs]," "booster clubs" for athletics, or other extra-curricular groups like the school choir, band, debate team, etc. In addition, local school boards will also hold public hearings from time to time on specific issues they are considering. Parents and other local citizens are invited to make public comments and to give advisory input, but that is as far as it goes. Once the "input" from local citizens has been heard, the school board and the administrators make all of the governing decisions and "outsiders" are not welcome or involved.

These kinds of committees, advisory groups and public hearings are purposely designed to provide the parents, students, community members, local government and business leaders with the *illusion* of involvement in the governance of local schools. When we get right down to it, however, engagement in the governance of local public school districts and schools is really "closed to outsiders."

It is important for Effective Action Teams to understand that when they are working to influence the governance policies and decisions of local school districts, it will be a difficult, uphill struggle. School district and school building administrators operate with an *internally-referenced* point of view and they are usually not open to meaningful participation by local citizens. Here are a couple of examples:

- The *curriculum* of the public schools (the subject areas of English, math, science, history, social studies, etc.), under federal and state laws, must include "common core content standards" which were developed by college and university professors, state level educational specialists, some K-12 teachers and administrators. The *curriculum* of the public schools, for the most part, is *not* open to include ideas from local citizens.

  Example: Under the federally-mandated laws of the *No Child Left Behind* (NCLB) national education program, the curriculum content standards are strongly focused on reading, writing, math, science and history/social studies. Any allocation of educational time for other subjects such as woodshop, auto shop, electronics, music, drama, debate, etc. is very restricted and not adequately funded.

- The teaching methods and teaching/learning processes of the public schools are also developed by college and university professors, educational researchers, teachers and some administrators. Here again, the processes are developed almost exclusively by professional educators and they are not open for the inclusion of ideas or suggestions from the local citizenry.

  Under the mandated rules of NCLB, teachers must use what are called "standardized teaching" methods-- primarily lectures, with some discussion and questioning. Any use of other teaching methods, such as hands-on learning or learning through performance and practice, are very limited and restricted.

- The *student achievement measurement processes* and the *student performance assessment and evaluation processes* use academic-standardized testing and other internal educational measurements, such as essays, quizzes, tests, etc., which are mandated by the federal and state governments. Again, suggestions from parents or other local citizens are not usually welcome.

  For example, under the mandated rules of NCLB, student grades must be calculated using only standardized test scores or assignments directly related to the NCLB academic content standards. Many school districts now use what are called "standards-based" report cards. Student grades *may not* be based on such things as student attendance, class participation, individual student progress or growth, student behaviors in class, etc.

- The *governance processes, procedures, regulations, rules* and *working relationships* are all developed and implemented from unique educational laws and policies which are used exclusively *inside* the bureaucracies of the public school systems. Inside school districts and schools, *administrative law and administrative regulations and procedures* prevail, and they are quite complex and *exclusive, i.e.,* local citizens have very little to say in these governance matters.

Example: Under the federally mandated rules of NCLB, teachers must be assigned to teach only in those areas for which they are properly credentialed. School districts may not assign teachers on the basis of their expertise in other career fields or in subject areas where they may have college or university work but do not have a credential. A person who has life-long experience with managing a local business may *not* teach high school business courses unless he or she has the proper credential.

- The *funding of the public schools and the financial management processes, procedures, regulations, rules* and *working relationships* are also developed and implemented from federal and state educational laws and policies. *Administrative regulations and procedures* which are used exclusively *inside* the bureaucracies of the public school systems. School district budgets, for example, are usually complex, and direct participation by local citizens in formulating these budgets is not welcome.

  Under the federally mandated rules of NCLB, local school districts must allocate both local and state educational funds for federally-mandated learning materials (textbooks, manuals, etc.), even if the local school districts have other learning materials which are still usable and state-approved.

What all of these *internally-referenced* examples and indicators tell us is that the managers (district and school administrators) and staff (bureaucrats) of K-12 public school districts are required to pay close attention to all of the state and federal laws, policies, regulations, procedures and rules. Moreover, the managers and staff of the K-12 public schools are required to become experts in understanding the unique bureaucratic language (nomenclature) that comes with all of these federal and state laws, policies, regulations, and rules, and they must have significant expertise in implementing them.

The public school managers (administrators) and staff (bureaucrats) are aware that the local citizenry doesn't know much about federal and state laws, policies, and rules so, in their managerial and bureaucratic minds, there is virtually no need to include the citizenry in the governance of the public schools, except perhaps some *pro forma* advisory committees or support groups.

Given these realities, it is fairly easy to see why public school districts are indeed a unique form of special districts. But what we have described so far is not the whole story. Public school districts occupy a unique place in our local governments because they are responsible for educating and preparing our children to successfully fulfill their adult roles and responsibilities in the 21st-century global economy and society. Local citizens have every right to inquire about the education of their children.

Moreover, the citizens in each local community, on a per capita basis and on a total overall basis, make a huge ongoing investment in our nation's public schools, to the tune of about $557 billion in 2007-2008. Estimates for spending on K-12 public education for FY 2009-2010 exceeded $750 billion, including federal, state and local tax dollars.[2]

When taxpayers in our local communities invest this much money in our K-12 public schools, they have every right to ask about their "Return on Investment." And they have every right to be active participants who are meaningfully engaged in the governance of their local school districts and schools. However, at this time, public involvement and engagement is difficult and very limited.

The world is changing rapidly and the rising performance requirements for jobs and careers in the 21st-century global economy continue to have great impact on our children and young adults. Competition for well-paying jobs and careers is becoming more challenging every day. Taxpayers and local citizens can and should use Effective Action Teams and the methods and techniques we described in Chapters 2 and 3 to influence the governance of their local public school districts, to ensure that their young people are being adequately prepared to achieve success in their future careers and adult lives.

In 2011, the average high school graduate earns an annual salary of $30,400, whereas those students who complete only some high school earn an average salary of only $23,400. And those who do well in high school and complete a Bachelor's degree earn an average annual salary of $52,200. All of these averages are based on one important assumption, however: that our high school and college graduates will be employed in meaningful, well-paying jobs.[3]

The pragmatic strategy, the seven "unwritten rules," the four tools and the fourteen steps for Effective Action Teams explained in Chapters 2 and 3 are critical for local citizens groups who want to effectively influence the governance of local schools. The ultimate goals of gaining "insider knowledge" and building long-term working relationships with local school district officials, managers and employees are essential because together they will secure the "leverage points" for sustained success. There are, however, some additional strategies which must be used when working with local school districts and schools, due to the unique closed and internally referenced governance structures, processes and working relationships we described above.

One unique challenge for citizens groups is due to what are called *reform programs* in local school districts and schools. Since the 1970s, American K-12 public school systems have been subjected to a veritable deluge of legally-*mandated* federal and state "reform programs," all designed to "improve" public education. This overwhelming flood of educational reform laws and regulations has created *three difficult realities* for citizens' groups who seek to effectively influence the governance of local schools:

1. The first difficulty is that decades of mandated reform programs have muddled the overall focus of public education. In earlier times, the educational purpose of our K-12 public schools was fairly clear and generally agreed upon: The public schools were to educate and prepare all students to be good citizens, to be literate and

to have the basic knowledge and skills necessary for success in their adult lives and careers.

Over time, this educational focus or purpose has been diluted with dozens of new federal and state government mandates. Here is a list of what our public schools are now required to provide:

- Free or reduced-price meals to students whose parents' incomes are below the poverty line.

- Instruction and training to prevent substance abuse, alcoholism, sexually transmitted diseases, and pregnancy.

- Training in how to deal with diverse ethnic, social, religious and cultural groups.

- Support for children and young adults who are the victims of parental abuse and neglect.

- Bilingual education for non-English speaking students.

- Instruction and training in first aid, CPR, and home health care.

- Education and training for students with physical, emotional and mental disabilities.

- Equal sports and athletics programs for boys and girls.

- Education and training in designated "common core content areas" in reading, mathematics, science and social studies, to prepare all students to achieve designated achievement targets on federally-mandated standardized tests.

- Education and training to prepare all students to go on to colleges or universities.

Each of these programs has merit, and they all add value to the lives and education of our children, but the organizational capacity of our public schools to provide all of these programs is simply inadequate. One example: When all of these programs emerged, starting in the 1970s, the annual public school year was 180 days in most states, and the length of the school day was 6.5 hours. By 2010, and the annual school year was still 180 days, and the school day was still 6.5 hours, but the number of state- and federally-mandated reform programs is greater than ever; and we have not even listed all the *curricular reform programs* added over the last three decades.

It should be noted that students in other nations typically have an annual school year between 190 days and 240 days in length, and their school days last usually 7.5 hours.

2. The second difficulty is that each of these federal and state mandated educational reform programs comes with its own set of laws, regulations, rules and procedures, and these then get translated into *administrative law* by the federal, state and local education bureaucrats. Also, the operational language or nomenclature is often esoteric, specialized and difficult for those outside of the educational bureaucracies to understand. Also, these federal and state mandated reform programs override virtually all local community priorities.

3. The third difficulty is that these federal and state programs *constantly change*. Over the past three decades, no fewer than thirty different curricular reform programs have come and gone, in addition to the broader programs listed in #1 above. These constant changes and seemingly endless cycles of change have left a residue of cynicism and negative attitudes about teachers and public school administrators, who then become defensive about the "involvement" or "participation" by local citizens' groups.

Effective Action Teams need to avoid getting bogged down in all of these mandated programs and focus instead on the larger goals of their local public school districts. Effective Action Teams should seek to have local school boards and school officials establish new processes to engage all of the *stakeholders* (students, parents, grandparents, business leaders, local government leaders, community leaders, etc.) in addressing two large, overriding questions:

- First, what are the common purposes everyone wants the local schools to implement for all of the students? These overriding purposes need to drive everything that happens in local school districts. For example: If one of the common purposes for public education is to make sure that ALL students graduate from high school well-educated and prepared for success in college and their adult lives, then what must be done locally to insure that this purpose is achieved? At the present time, 30% of American students *fail* to graduate from high school in the majority of states.

- Second, what knowledge, skills, attitudes and behaviors do all students need to learn, apply and master, in order to successfully fulfill their adult roles and responsibilities in the 21st-century global economy and society?

To answer these questions, the local citizens (stakeholders), hopefully working in Effective Action Teams, school administrators and teachers should work together to conduct research, hold public meetings and communicate with the business leaders, government and community leaders who know the learning requirements and performance expectations for students to succeed in their future adult lives and careers.

Such processes may lead to potential conflicts between the educational priorities of local citizens, employers and other stakeholders, and those mandated by federal and state laws. For example, we surveyed business leaders who will employ our future high school and college graduates, and here are some of the *Essential Knowledge, Skills, Attitudes and Behaviors* (EKSABs) they identified as having high priority:

- Public speaking and high level verbal communication skills.

- Delivering excellent customer service.

- Being on time, dependable, responsible and accountable.

- Being self-directed, taking the initiative to see what needs to be done and then doing those things without being asked.

- Having high-level technical skills and the ability to use computers, the Internet, and a wide variety of software applications.

- Having excellent technical writing skills, spelling skills, and grammar usage skills.

- Knowing how to work with diverse types of people in effective teams.

- Knowing how to plan, develop, implement and manage complex projects.

- Having excellent time-management skills and a commitment to doing whatever it takes to make the company successful and the customers happy.

- Having excellent skills in applied mathematics, estimating, accounting, budgeting, etc.

Where do we find these skills in the K-12 curricula or courses? In many cases, they simply are not there. But they could be included in K-12 curricula and courses, if they are properly integrated with the state and federal curricular content standards. Many school districts have career pathways or academies which integrate the state and federal learning standards with the standards required by colleges, universities, local and regional employers. Parents and other local citizens working in Effective Action Teams can make it happen.

For example, every high school graduate should be taught how to manage his or her personal finances (how to manage a savings account, a checking account, credit cards), and how to deal effectively with such financial issues as buying and maintaining a car, paying for college, renting an apartment, paying taxes, investing, etc.). In most American high schools, education in personal finances is inadequate and most high school graduates know very little about this critical skill set.

Effective Action Teams should also insist that stakeholder engagement events be established as ongoing governance *processes* and not just one-time events. Local school districts should re-visit their mission statements each year, and perform annual updates on Essential Knowledge, Skills, Attitudes and Behaviors (EKSABs) requirements, using new research and updated information from employers, businesses, local government leaders, community leaders, colleges and universities, and career or job training institutions.

In addition focusing on the commonly-agreed purposes and Essential Knowledge, Skills, Attitudes and Behaviors (EKSABs) to be mastered by all K-12 graduates, Effective Action Teams should also place consider five other "high leverage" areas of local school district governance:

1.   School district revenue sources (local property taxes or other local taxes, state funding allocations and federal funding allocations) and the prioritization of how school funds are used to implement the agreed-upon purposes, education and preparation of all students in the Essential Knowledge, Skills, Attitudes and Behaviors (EKSABs). School district budgets, by law, are public documents which must be made available to the citizens. Effective Action Teams should obtain copies of school district budgets, and the budgets for each individual school, and study them carefully. It would help to solicit expert advice from experienced educators (consultants) who are familiar with the specialized terminology of these budget documents. Local citizens' groups cannot force local school districts to *override* federal and state funding mandates, but they can influence the districts to use federal, state and local education funds with a much stronger focus on the EKSABs.

2.   Study school district employee staffing allocations and the prioritization of school district spending on hiring and training teachers, administrators, counselors, support staff members, and "classified" employees (bus drivers, custodians, maintenance workers, cafeteria workers, secretaries, teacher aides). In most public school districts, about 85% of the total budget is spent on people's salaries, so the prioritization of these expenditures is critical to school district governance. Effective Action Teams should work with local school boards and

administrators to create processes that engage local stakeholders in establishing employee staffing funding allocation each school year and within larger five-year plans.

3.   The heart of any effective and successful educational process comes down to the relationships between the teachers and the students. Well-trained, energetic, high-quality teachers who engage, motivate, challenge, discipline, support and nurture students are critical to learning success. Effective Action Teams need to focus on working with school administrators and teachers to understand the whole process for assessing and evaluating teacher performances and administrator performances. Effective Action Teams should also help establish new processes, whereby the input from students, parents and other stakeholders is included in those assessments and evaluations. There are certain legal restrictions on the assessment and evaluation processes which protect the privacy and legal rights of teachers and administrators, but there are also adequate provisions in the laws to include input from parents and other local citizens.

4.   School districts, as noted above, are virtually buried in federal- and state-mandated education reform programs, but the processes for implementing these programs can and should be more open, transparent and better integrated and coordinated. Effective Action Teams should focus on getting school district administrators to establish governance teams at the district level and at the school building level, to work collaboratively with local citizens to understand these programs, to prioritize the work and to coordinate the work with the priorities of the local citizenry.

5.   Since 2001, school districts have been under a daunting federal mandate from the *No Child Left Behind* (NCLB) program. NCLB requires all school districts to conduct annual cycles of standardized testing to measure student achievements in reading,

writing, mathematics, science and history/social studies. The students' test scores are then statistically aggregated for each school into derived index rankings called *Annual Yearly Progress (AYP)* reports. Schools who meet their *AYP* targets are commended, and schools that do not are placed in a probationary status known as "Program Improvement," or P.I. When a school is in P.I. status, parents have the legal authority to request that their children be transferred to other schools, including private schools. If a school does not improve and remains in P.I. status for three years, the school may be completely restructured or closed.

Effective Action Teams should focus on greater parental and stakeholder involvement in NCLB testing and test preparation process, and should also work with administrators and teachers to broaden the processes for evaluating student achievements beyond standardized testing so that learning Essential Knowledge, Skills, Attitudes and Behaviors (EKSABs) are also measured.

In summary, the pragmatic strategy, the seven "unwritten rules," the four tools and the fourteen steps for Effective Action Teams explained in Chapters 2 and 3 should be used when dealing with the governance of school districts and schools, bearing in mind the unique areas of focus described above.

We would also add one final caveat: Effective Action Teams need to take care to avoid the internal political conflicts which exist in most K-12 public school districts, to wit:

- Conflicts between school boards and district administrators.
- Conflicts between school boards and teachers' unions or classified employees' unions.
- Conflicts between school boards and local business, governmental and community leaders.
- Conflicts between district administrators and teachers' unions and/or classified employees' unions.

Effective Action Teams should focus on the "high leverage" governance areas described above and should always emphasize top-quality student learning, student achievement and student performances of the Essential Knowledge, Skills, Attitudes and Behaviors (EKSABs). By doing so, Effective Action Teams will avoid the typical kinds of internal conflicts noted above. Those conflicts are usually about what is best for the adults, not what is best for the students.

Local K-12 public school districts, as unique forms of special districts, are one of the hardest areas of local government for citizens' groups to influence because, as we have explained, they are closed systems and they usually do not welcome active participation by local citizens in their governance processes. But using our strategies, tools and methods, Effective Action Teams can achieve some measure of success in opening up and influencing the governance of local school districts and schools. Such work is challenging and difficult, but the future of our children and young adults depends on the active involvement of local citizens in school districts.

Chapter 5

Local Court Systems

Local governments in all fifty states include local court or judiciary systems. Most Americans have seen TV shows such as *"Law and Order," "Judge Judy," "The People's Court"* or *"Divorce Court,"* or older courtroom dramas like *"Perry Mason,"* but these television shows do not tell the whole story of the realities of court systems. Also, and most importantly, these shows do not provide the information which is essential for local citizens' groups to effectively influence local government through their local courts. Local court systems have tremendous political power and leverage over local governments so it is imperative for EATS to understand how local court systems operate.

In most states, the local court systems include courts which operate at the county or parish level of local government, and courts which operate at the municipal level of local government in cities, towns and villages. These local court systems are part of a larger statewide court system in each state, which includes appellate courts and, typically, a state supreme court. These local courts handle the following general types of legal actions[1]:

- Major criminal cases, including felonies and serious misdemeanors
- Minor criminal cases, including infractions (ordinance violations), traffic citations, etc.
- Major civil cases involving torts, contracts, real property, probate/estate cases, domestic relations, etc. which exceed monetary amounts of $10,000 to $25,000, or higher

- Minor civil cases dealing with small claims, typically in amounts not exceeding $10,000

- Juvenile criminal cases, domestic relations cases, truancy, etc.

The organizational structure of the county level courts is established by the state government, and is set up by judicial circuits or districts, or on a county-by-county basis. In states with smaller populations, the county level judicial circuits or districts are typically geographic areas encompassing two or more counties or portions thereof.

In Alabama, for example, there are two kinds of county level courts: Circuit Courts, which handle major criminal and civil cases in 41 geographic areas known as circuits, and District Courts, which handle misdemeanor criminal cases and smaller civil cases, juvenile cases and traffic infractions, in 67 geographic areas called districts. By comparison, in California, the county level courts are called Superior Courts and there is one Superior Court in each of California's 58 counties, which handles both major and minor criminal and civil cases.

At the municipal level in each state, there are a variety of lower level courts in cities, towns and villages. The names vary in each state: Municipal Courts, Justice of the Peace Courts, City Courts, Alderman's Courts, Magistrate Courts, etc. Typically, these courts do not have jury trials or any major criminal or civil cases. They handle minor criminal cases (misdemeanors, infractions, traffic citations) and minor civil cases (domestic relations, small claims, small civil suits, juvenile cases, mental health cases, preliminary hearings).

In addition to the county-level courts and municipal-level courts in local systems, each of the states has a number of specialized courts or other judicial entities and these include[2]:

- Probate Courts: These courts handle only civil cases relating to the ownership of estates which include property or other assets, trusts, wills, adoptions, some mental health cases, etc.

- Juvenile Courts: These courts handle only criminal or civil cases relating to children under the age of 18.

- Traffic Courts: These courts handle only minor traffic cases, parking tickets, etc.

- Tax Courts: These are administrative law courts and they hear appeals by individuals who are dealing with administrative agencies, typically at the county/parish or municipal level.

- Water Courts: These are courts that deal exclusively with civil cases relating to real property cases involving water rights or domestic or agricultural water systems.

- Family Court: These handle low level domestic relations issues, some misdemeanors, juvenile issues or traffic infractions.

- Grand Juries: These are special judicial entities made up of local citizens who are appointed to serve by judges in the Circuit Courts or Superior Courts. Grand Juries are usually composed of 12 to 20 local citizens and they have two major functions: [1] to issue criminal indictments (formal criminal charges) in major criminal cases; and [2] to conduct formal investigations into the operations of all aspects of local government.

- Indian Tribal Courts and Courts of Tribal Offenses: These are very specialized courts that operate at the local level on Indian reservations but they are in fact part of the federal court system.

    Note: Tribal courts are operated by Indian tribes under laws and procedures that the Tribe has enacted or made one of their laws, and they often differ from the laws and procedures in federal and state courts. Most Tribes receive funding from the Department of the Interior to operate their court systems, although many supplement this funding with their own resources. Courts of Indian Offenses are courts operated on certain reservations by the Department of the Interior, Bureau of Indian Affairs. Those courts operate under federal regulations contained in Volume 25 of the Code of Federal Regulations and, for this reason, are often referred to as "CFR" courts. At present, there are approximately 150 tribal courts in operation in the United States and approximately 20 CFR courts.

We have purposely left the local court systems by citizens as the last major area in this book because the use of local courts to influence local government should be an option of last resort.

When local citizens have formed Effective Action Teams and have utilized our seven "unwritten rules," the four "tools" and the fourteen steps, and they have maximized the use of *leverage points* to influence county or parish governments, city or town governments, special district or school district governments, and they still have not achieved their intended goals, then their efforts might require an action in the local courts. We would issue a strong word of caution here, however, because what we are about to discuss are civil claims and lawsuits, and these court actions are usually expensive and consume a lot of time and energy.

It is usually correct to assume that when citizens' groups (hopefully in Effective Action Teams) decide to take legal action in their local courts, they are unfamiliar with the whole process of civil claims and lawsuits, so we advise that the first step should be to secure competent legal counsel. Citizens who try to carry out civil claims or lawsuits themselves, without the guidance and services of well-qualified attorneys, are just asking for trouble and their efforts often end in failure.

The good news is that the same research methods we described in Chapter 1 and 2 can be used to research attorneys, and Effective Action Teams will already have their research people and processes in place. When Effective Action Teams are deciding whether or not to use the local courts to achieve their goals, they should always make such decisions with the guidance of competent and reputable lawyers.

Here are some recommended action steps which all Effective Action Teams should implement if they are going to pursue civil claims or lawsuits in the local courts:

1. **Start by assuming that your Effective Action Team knows virtually nothing** about civil claims or lawsuits, even if certain members of your team actually do know some things. In the arena of the local courts, what you don't know can really hurt you, and judges will rarely cut you any slack just because your group is ignorant of how the local courts operate.

2. **Conduct a thorough research process into available local attorneys** (we will use the terms *attorneys* and *lawyers* interchangeably) including checking on their reputations and how well they have performed for past clients. Also, focus your research on attorneys or lawyers who have the expertise your EAT will need relative to the goals and objectives you are pursuing. For example, If your EAT is working to get some specific action with a school district, then you will need an attorney who has expert knowledge in education laws, codes, rules and regulations, in addition to being an expert on civil claims and lawsuits.

3. **Your Effective Action Team should be prepared to pay** for the initial consultation sessions with the attorney you ultimately select, to review, analyze and evaluate the facts and evidence in your claim(s) or intended lawsuit. This means your EAT will have to do some fund-raising before you select your attorney and do the initial consultation. Also, your Effective Action Team should discuss its commitment to perform the ongoing fund-raising which will be necessary to pay for your attorney and court costs. *Civil claims and lawsuits are expensive and your EAT must be prepared to have the required funds on hand and to do more fund-raising over several months or years if necessary.*

4. **When you have selected an attorney to work with your EAT, the next step is to meet with him or her to thoroughly discuss the facts and evidence** in the case. Local court procedures and processes are important to understand but the major focus of your EAT should be on the facts (solid, substantiated, accurate information) and evidence (conclusions that may be inferred without positive statements of facts or circumstances) at the core of your claim(s) or intended lawsuit.

    Here again, if your Effective Action Team has used the seven "unwritten rules," the four "tools" and the fourteen steps, then you already know the *leverage points* to influence local government, and your team will already have identified and documented the facts and/or evidence you will need for a successful civil claim and/or lawsuit.

Also, competent, skilled, experienced attorneys will almost always work with your EAT to do a thorough analysis and evaluation of the facts and evidence before advising you on whether or not you should pursue your civil claims or a lawsuit in the local courts.

In short: If the proper facts and evidence are NOT present or are not sufficient, then all the fancy legal maneuverings in the world will not help your team. Start with the facts and stick to the facts and/or *strong evidence*, and your chances of success will be significantly greater.

5.   Once your Effective Action Team has its initial consultation with the attorney or attorneys, **the next step is to have a conversation with the attorney(s) to get a realistic understanding of your chances of success in pursuing civil claims or a lawsuit.** It is important to understand that "justice" and "legal rights" are, in almost all cases, only what a particular judge says they are. There is nothing wrong with pursuing justice as an ideal goal but, in most civil claims or lawsuits, justice is not the issue. The issue is this: Do you have the facts and/or evidence you need to support your civil claim or lawsuit, *and* can those facts and/or *evidence* be successfully presented to and accepted by the judge? Knowing the truth and proving it in court are two very different things.

6.   **Have your attorney help you figure out which court has *jurisdiction* over the civil claim(s) or lawsuit your EAT intends to pursue.** *Jurisdiction* refers to the specific legal authority of a particular court to hear and act on your civil claim or lawsuit. As noted in the introductory pages of this chapter, most significant civil claims or lawsuits involving more than $25,000 will be held in the higher levels of county, parish, circuit or

district courts in your area, and your attorney will know which particular court has *jurisdiction*.

7. **After the proper court with *jurisdiction* has been identified, the next step is for the EAT to work with its attorney to evaluate the available judges to whom your case may be assigned.** It is no secret to the attorneys that certain judges are easier to work with and more effective with certain types of cases, and it is very important to get your civil claim or lawsuit heard by the best possible judge, one who will be the most helpful and effective in understanding your goals and objectives. If possible, your EAT should avoid having your civil claim or lawsuit adjudicated by a judge who may be hostile to your goals Judges are human beings just like the rest of us and, while they are supposed to uphold the principles of fairness and objectivity, they usually lean a little bit in favor of or against certain groups or issues.

8. **Work with your attorney to get a thorough understanding of the *total process* and *total scope* of your intended civil claim or lawsuit.** Your EAT will need to have a clear, well-defined and carefully-described picture of what the case will involve, including the use of expert witnesses, other court processes, motions, appeals, etc., as well as how long the case will take, and what the total estimated costs will be.

9. In understanding the *total process* and *total scope* of what is required to succeed in your civil claim(s) or lawsuit, it is **important for your Effective Action Team to have a solid internal agreement on what your group is willing to accept if your case involves a legal settlement, *and* what your citizens group is willing to give up** to obtain a legal settlement. By the same token, it is important to know what your group is willing to accept or give up in order to go all the way to a civil jury trial to reach your goals. As your attorney will explain, civil jury trials are often long, complicated

and expensive, and the outcome is often uncertain, so your EAT should be prepared to accept a legal settlement before going to trial, if that is the best you can do at a given point in time.

10. **Finally, it is very important for all the members of your Effective Action Team to do their homework.** Every member of your citizens' group needs to ramp up their knowledge about local court procedures, practices, rules, traditions and rituals. The judges, clerks, bailiffs and other staff members in local courts have certain ways of doing things, and the members of your EAT will need to learn them. Also, the members of your EAT will need to sincerely adopt a working philosophy and attitude which is courteous, respectful and reserved. Almost all local judges regard their courtrooms as places where they are in total control, and their directives are not to be questioned or challenged. They will not tolerate audience comments or outbursts, and they will not look kindly on anyone in your group who acts in an immature, uninformed or less than professional manner. Here are some helpful guidelines which all members of your EAT must follow in order to achieve a favorable ruling from local court judges:

- Always be on time--in fact, always arrive early. Judges run their courts on strict schedules and they do not care if your group members were stuck in traffic, missed their train, took the wrong subway or had problems parking. Coming into court late is a big "NO NO."

- Let your attorney(s) do most of the work. They know the procedures, rules, practices, traditions and rituals, AND they know the judges. In 99% of communications with the local court judges, unless you are called upon to speak, let your attorney(s) do the talking.

- If someone in your group has a question during the court proceedings, quietly pass a note to your attorney(s) or to the group members who are seated near to the attorney(s). Communicate verbally in low, whispered tones and never talk when the judge, clerk or other staff members are speaking.

- In courtrooms and in the hallways and offices near courtrooms, always be on your best behavior and remember that there are no such things as "casual conversations." Members of your EAT should never discuss anything about your case in public, because you never know who might be listening. Wait until you are in a private, secure location to discuss your case, and do not discuss your case on the phone.

- Do not have any e-mail communications among the members of your team about your court case. E-mails can be used as evidence against you.

- Do not have any conversations with the attorneys or lawyers who represent the opposing side (county government, city or town government, special districts or school districts) or with any members of their staffs or with any employees of the local government entity involved in your case. Also, do not have any conversations with any members of the jury if you are involved in jury trial or with any of the witnesses used by the opposing side.

- Members of your EAT should never talk with the local media, or any other media, for that matter. Let your attorney(s) do the talking with the media, if they think it is necessary. When in doubt, just say "no comment" or say nothing, even if reporters are hounding you with rude and intrusive questions. Local court judges will get very angry if they feel that members of your group are "trying the case in the press."

- Dress neatly and in business attire. A local court is not your living room or your local bar; it is a formal place of business, so you need to dress and behave appropriately. Tank tops, low-cut or see-through blouses, short skirts, flip-flops, "sagging" jeans, baseball caps or other casual dress items are not acceptable in courts.

- Remember that your local courts deal with criminal cases and individuals who are not the nicest people to be around, so they are very concerned with *security*. In most court houses these days, members of your group should expect to be screened through a metal detector and to have bags, purses, and briefcases opened and inspected. Common sense dictates that members of your EAT should not bring anything into the court facility which could even remotely be considered a security problem, such as guns, knives (even small pocket knives), mace, or any other items which can be considered as potential weapons. Have your identification documents (driver's license, passport, green card, etc.) ready to present them. And, for goodness' sake, do not bring any drugs or alcohol into a court facility.

- One final note: Bring items related to the case which you can study, bring books to read, and bring a notepad and pens because you will spend plenty of time waiting in the courtroom or in the hallways, and you will need to take notes during the court proceedings.

What we now have in place are the practical professional rules for local citizens' groups (hopefully working in Effective Action Teams) to follow when they decide to pursue civil claims or lawsuits in order to influence some specific part of local government. In addition to these practical professional rules, it is important for local citizens' groups to learn the fundamentals of the "language" or nomenclature which is used in local courts. We have all heard the term "legalese," which is generally used in a derogatory way to criticize the technical language which is used by lawyers and judges. And we most likely have heard something like "so and so lost his case because of a *technicality.*" These sorts of complaints are usually made by people who do not fully understand courtroom or legal processes. On the one hand,

America is by far the leading nation when it comes to lawsuits, restraining orders, civil claims, etc., but on the other hand, there is a strong American tradition of distrusting lawyers and fancy legal "mumbo jumbo."

As Americans, we are blessed with a strong legal tradition and legal protections which are embedded in the document which is the source of all government in the United States, namely, our Constitution. The constitutions of each of the fifty states, as well as local county and city charters must be in alignment with the U.S. *Constitution.* It is not the purpose of this book to provide our readers with a course in constitutional law, or an in-depth analysis of our legal systems. It is our purpose to provide citizens and groups with sufficient technical knowledge so they can be effective in using the local courts to influence local government. With this context in mind, here are some key technical terms and definitions which all Effective Action Teams should know and use when working with their attorneys and local courts[3]:

- *Parties*: The people involved in civil cases--civil claims, restraining orders, lawsuits, etc.--are referred to as the "parties" in the case. The two opposing sides are referred to as *Plaintiffs* and *Defendants*. The *Plaintiffs* are those who are bringing the legal action, such as a lawsuit to obtain compensation for injury or damages, or a lawsuit to force some agency or entity of local government to do something. The *Defendants* are those who are being sued or who are allegedly at fault for causing injury or damages, or perhaps those in local government who are opposed to doing what a particular citizens' group wants them to do.

- *Pleadings*: These are formal statements or allegations by the parties to an action (typically a lawsuit or petition to the court) to present the operative facts which constitute the basis for their respective claims (e.g., the city government is not properly maintaining playgrounds for local children) or defenses (the parks and recreation department presents information to substantiate that the playgrounds are safe for children). The *pleadings* also describe the key points in the dispute between the parties.

- *Proceeding*: The form and process for conducting judicial business before a court or judicial officer (such as a judge) and any application made to the court for aid in the enforcement of rights, for relief or redress of injuries or damages, or for any remedial action (such as a lawsuit, civil claim or petition for a restraining order). There are three types of proceedings:

  a) *Ordinary proceedings* which, as the name suggests, are the regular and usual modes of doing business in a court.

  b) *Special proceedings*, which are specific court processes specified in law (federal or state statutes) for a certain kind of problem. For example, a lawsuit by a citizens' group about an environmental issue may require a special proceeding before a court that deals with such issues or problems.

  c) *Summary proceedings*, which are a form of court trial in which the ordinary proceedings are discarded and the judge, after proper investigation and presentation of the facts and evidence, makes a final ruling. Some typical cases here might involve recovery of property leased to a tenant, actions to abate a public nuisance, enforcement of a municipal ordinance, or action to remove a public (local government) officer.

- *Cause of Action*: This refers to the right of a party (an individual or group) to institute a judicial proceeding. A *cause of action* also includes a set of facts which is claimed to have caused a wrongful injury to a person or persons and which entitles the injured or damaged person to relief (financial compensation or some other actions to correct the injury or the damage). A *cause of action* cannot exist without the existence of some legal right, duty or omission. For example, in order for a citizens' group to sue a city government to force the city to install safer playgrounds, there must be some legal right which has been violated (perhaps safety laws) or some duty (city officials have a duty to protect children and keep them safe) or some omission (city officials and employees failed to install proper safety padding under the play equipment in the park).

- *Right of Action*: A *right of action* is usually a ruling by a judge which gives one of the parties the right to proceed with a *cause of action.* One example might be a judge's ruling that a group of citizens has the legal right to sue a county government over some issue or problem for which the citizens' group is seeking redress or remedy (typically some action by local government to correct a problem, to change its practices or procedures, or to pay damages for harm to someone or to property).

- *Action*: An *action* refers to a process such as a civil claim, lawsuit or petition for the court to order something done or something stopped.

- *Trial*: This is the court proceeding to investigate and determine the issues and facts in a case, either civil (like a lawsuit) or criminal (where a defendant is accused of a crime).

- *Venue*: the *venue* for a court proceeding is the actual physical place where the processes take place. We often hear about a criminal defendant's attorney making a motion for a *change of venue*. This is a formal request to the judge to move the criminal trial to a different location, usually another city or county.

- In civil cases such as lawsuits by citizens' groups, the court has several options for making a final ruling:

    a) *Judgment*: This is a legal conclusion based on the pleadings, facts and evidence presented during the court proceedings. The judge or, in some cases, the jury, will make a ruling or *judgment,* usually in favor of either the plaintiff or the defendant in a civil case.

    b) An *order*: An *order* is a specific ruling by a judge to grant relief or to deny relief to one of the parties.

This usually happens in a case where there are *special proceedings*. An *order* can also legally confirm a *settlement* (mutual agreement) which both parties agree to before or during a civil proceeding.

c) A *dispute resolution*: A *dispute resolution* is process for attempting to resolve the issues in a conflict between two parties *before* any other formal legal actions, like a lawsuit, are taken. Most *dispute resolutions* are *non-adversarial*, meaning that they are done through mediation and a neutral third party is brought in to help the conflicting parties come to a workable resolution of their problems.

• *Contempt of Court*: Any conduct in court by the parties which constitutes an offense against the authority and dignity of the court or judicial officer (usually a judge). In most civil cases, *contempt of court* occurs when one of the parties acts or fails to act as ordered to do by the judge. For example: The judge hearing a lawsuit case orders one of the parties to produce certain documents relevant to the lawsuit, and the party does not produce them. This party can be charged with *civil contempt of court,* and the judge can sanction (punish) them in some manner, like paying a fine or paying the court costs for the opposing party, etc. In criminal cases, if one of the defendants or witnesses does something which violates or offends the authority and dignity of the court, that person can be held in *criminal contempt of court,* which can result in the judge ordering them to serve time in jail, in addition to paying fines.

• *Burden of Proof*: This refers to the responsibility for one party in a court case to present enough facts and evidence to prove that his or her case is true, valid and accurate. In civil cases, the *burden of proof* is judged by a *preponderance of the evidence*, i.e., in the final analysis, there is sufficient evidence or facts to demonstrate a very strong likelihood that the allegations by the party are true, correct and valid. In criminal cases, the "state" (usually represented by the local District

Attorney or one of the Assistant District Attorneys) must prove that the defendant is guilty and must show that the facts and evidence demonstrate the defendant's guilt *beyond the shadow of a doubt.* This means that if the jury or the judge in a criminal trial has any significant doubts about the facts or evidence, then the defendant must be found *not guilty.*

It is important for citizens' groups to understand that when they take action in local court to compel local government entities to do something, in almost all cases, the *burden of proof* rests on those who are bringing the civil action. And it is equally important for citizens' groups to understand that *knowing the truth* about some issue or problem and *proving the truth in court* are two very different things.

The facts or evidence in a given case are not *legally accepted* as "facts" or "evidence" until the judge says they are. In both civil and criminal cases, there are *rules of evidence* which the judge must follow in determining if something presented is legally acceptable in a specific case.

For example, let's say that members of a citizens' group sneak into the office of some local government official to make copies of certain documents before replacing them. This would be a very stupid thing to do, because it is a criminal act, for starters, and also because the judge is going to ask how they obtained the copies, and how the citizens' group can prove that the copies are authentic and valid. Because these documents were obtained illegally, the judge would not allow them to be entered into the facts and evidence in the case *even though the documents may show that a particular government official has acted in ways which are illegal or even criminal.*

We have all seen TV shows where the evidence against a certain criminal defendant is thrown out by the judge because the police or sheriff or FBI agents obtained the evidence without a proper search warrant or proper judicial order.

- *Statute of Limitations*: A statute is a law established by the federal government or a state government. A *statute of limitations* is a law which establishes specific time limits on certain crimes or civil rights of citizens or groups to bring a civil action against government officials or local entities. Some common examples here include a time limit on the number of years when certain lawsuits are allowed. If the city government failed to repair a certain street and someone's car was damaged as a result, and the owner of the car did not take any civil action until five years later, then the *statute of limitations* may prevent the car owner from taking any action. Or, in criminal cases, charges against a defendant must be filed within a certain number of years after the crime is alleged to have occurred. If the charges are not filed within those time limits, then they can never be filed. Citizens' groups are strongly advised to work with their attorney to identify the *statute of limitations* on any civil actions they intend to take to influence local government.

- *Common Law*: *Common Law* refers to "law" that is created by court decisions or rulings by administrative law judges. *Common laws* are usually unwritten and based on certain legal rules or principles and on a judge's innate sense of justice. *Common law* varies from state to state and from locality to locality.

In addition to taking the civil actions describe above, citizens and citizens' groups can work through the local court systems to influence local government in other ways.

Electing Local Judges

In most states, local court judges are elected by the voters in non-partisan elections, and they serve terms in office which vary between four and ten years. Local citizens' groups (especially if they work in Effective Action Teams) can be very effective in running or working in campaigns to elect (or to unseat) local judges. By using the information they gather, and the working relationships they establish with local government managers and employees (*leverage points*), Effective Action Teams can have a strong and consistent influence on the outcome of local elections of judges.

Serving on Grand Juries

Local citizens, as members of citizens' groups, can influence local government in another way when they serve on *Grand Juries*. Most states have Grand Juries which are made up of anywhere from twelve to twenty-five local citizens who apply to serve on the Grand Jury and are appointed to serve, usually by a county level judge.

Grand Juries are usually established by each county or parish and their powers and procedures are determined by state laws. In almost all of the states which have Grand Juries, the Grand Juries are empowered to investigate the management, operations and financial records of county or parish governments, cities, towns, special districts and school districts. Grand Juries are not legally empowered to investigate individual citizens or individual government officials, nor are they allowed to investigate state or federal agencies.

Grand Juries usually operate through one of three basic processes. First, they have the power to investigate written complaints from citizens. Second, Grand Juries can initiate investigations in response to written "inquiries" proposed by one or more members of a given Grand Jury. Third, Grand Juries have the power to investigate the management, operations and financial records of local government entities. In order to take action using these three methods, a proper quorum of the members of the Grand Jury (usually 50% of the total number of Grand Jurors plus one) must be physically present before the vote can be taken, and then a majority of those members must vote in favor of the proposed investigation.

Written complaints by local citizens and "inquiries" written by members of a Grand Jury must be submitted in the required format established by state law. These must be based on facts and/or evidence which are obtained from authentic, valid and accurate sources of information. Grand Juries may not engage in or respond to rumors or innuendos and they may not meddle indiscriminately in the affairs of local government. Also, members of Grand Juries may not engage in investigating their own personal "hidden agendas."

In addition to these two investigative processes, most Grand Juries are also empowered to hear reports from various department officials in local government on an annual basis, and to interview the leaders or officials to clarify what is going on in their departments or other areas of local government.

At the end of their investigations and information-gathering, Grand Juries prepare and submit an annual Grand Jury Report to the county level judge who supervises their work, to the county governing body (usually the County Board of Supervisors), and to the public. In these reports, Grand Juries describe their findings and also state specific actions to correct any problems they find or to improve certain situations or conditions or issues they identify. Then, during the subsequent year, local government department leaders or officials must respond to these directive actions and must prepare written reports for the next Grand Jury to substantiate what they have done to carry out these actions or to explain why they have not done so.

In addition to these investigative powers, Grand Juries in some states are also involved in county-level criminal processes. Local District Attorneys present witnesses, facts and other evidence to Grand Juries in order to obtain *criminal indictments* (statements of formal criminal charges) against a person or persons who stand accused of committing a crime. If a Grand Jury votes to issue what is often called a "true bill" of criminal charges, then the person or persons involved are formally charged (indicted) with a crime or multiple crimes, and they are then "bound over" for a criminal trial in a circuit court, district court, or county superior court. The use of Grand Juries to obtain *criminal indictments* has declined over the years, and most District Attorneys now engage in *preliminary hearings* before a judge, whereby the essential facts and evidence against someone accused of a crime are presented to the county-level judge, who then orders a criminal trial or takes some other legal action or dismisses the charges against the defendant.

Members of a Grand Jury cannot bring criminal charges against an individual or several people by themselves; the criminal charges, facts, evidence and witnesses must be brought to them by the District Attorney. In the course of carrying out their regular annual investigations of citizen complaints, Grand Juror inquiries, or their regular annual assessments of local government departments or functions, a Grand Jury may ascertain that criminal activities may have occurred, in which case they must present this information to the judge and District Attorney, who then decide if any criminal investigations should be conducted or if criminal charges should be brought against certain individuals.

Local Court Service

The third and final course of action for individual citizens or groups of citizens to use the local courts to influence local government involves service to the court system, working directly with the police, sheriff or other officers of the local courts.

Service to the local court system, or *jury duty* as it is known in most states, is required by law for all United States citizens who reside in a local area for at least a year. County courts have processes whereby the names of citizens are identified from lists of people who are registered to vote, or who have obtained a driver's license, or who have taken other official actions with local government such as obtain a business license. Each citizen is then sent a *juror summons* by the county court, which requires him or her to report to the court on a certain date to potentially serve on a jury or juries in civil or criminal cases.

Most courts have processes whereby individual citizens can file a written request to *postpone* their jury service if the *juror summons* happens to fall at a time when they have already paid for an airline flight or a vacation or when they are required to be present in some other legal action like a divorce or probate hearing or juvenile hearing, etc.

Prospective jurors can also be *officially excused* from jury service by the judge if they have certain conditions or situations which would prevent them from rendering proper and objective decisions in civil or criminal trials. Typically these conditions or situations include:

- Actual or potential conflicts of interest. These are situations where a prospective juror is related to the defendant in a criminal case, a witness in a criminal or civil case, one of the parties to a civil action, or one of the attorneys, the judge or other court official.

- Actual or potential issues with the ability of the prospective juror to render a fair and unbiased judgment in a given case because he or she regularly works with the police or sheriff's office, or with certain businesses or government agencies which would be involved in one particular side in a civil action.

- Legitimate individual personal issues or situations such as health conditions which would prevent full and complete attention or would limit the ability of the potential juror to serve, family conditions or situations where the potential juror must provide childcare or care for elderly parents or relatives, or individual religious or political views which would prevent a potential juror from rendering a fair, objective and unbiased decision in a civil or criminal trial.

Some people view jury service as an imposition on their lives or as some sort of negative experience, but these views, while understandable in some cases, are usually incorrect. Participating in the jury service process provides each individual with a powerful set of learning opportunities and the knowledge obtained is usually very helpful in subsequent efforts to influence local government. Effective Action Teams should encourage their members to participate in the jury service process as another way to identify and gain access to key *leverage points* to influence local government.

Participating in jury service is not only a duty for each American citizen, it also provides the following learning benefits:

- Citizens get to observe the operations of their local courts in an "up close and personal" way.

- Citizens get to participate in the process of juror selection for civil or criminal trials, and to participate in, or observe, what is called the *voir dire* examination of prospective jurors by the attorneys for both sides. The *voir dire* process involves the attorneys (and sometimes the judge) asking questions of prospective jurors to determine if they can make decisions which are fair and objective after hearing all of the testimony and seeing all of the facts and evidence. The purpose of the process is to eliminate any prospective jurors who may have conflicts of interest, or may be prejudiced or biased, or may have religious or political beliefs which prevent them from rendering a fair and objective decision.

- Citizens who are actually selected to serve on juries get to participate in a civil or criminal trial process and learn all of the actual elements of how local trial processes work and what they include.

- Citizens get to know more about local judges and attorneys.

- Citizens learn more about certain expert witnesses and other local government officials.

- Citizens meet other local people whom they might otherwise never meet, and they get to learn new perspectives, insights and understandings about local government, including the local courts.

In addition to jury service, local citizens or citizens' groups can also work directly with the local courts or local government agencies or departments which regularly work with the local courts, such as the police department, sheriff's department, the probation department, social services department, juvenile courts, child protective services, and other agencies.

Here, again, Effective Action Teams have opportunities to get to know local government managers and employees, to establish professional working relationships with them, and to build networks of relationships which lead to more *leverage points* to influence local government. Some of the typical programs which are present in most local communities or counties include:

- Police or Sheriff's "ride along" programs, where local citizens can ride with the police or sheriff's officers while they are on patrol or carrying out other duties.

- Police, Sheriff's or Fire Department auxiliary support groups.

- Juvenile offender "peer court" programs, where high school age students serve on "juries" and work with county level judges to go through court hearings for low level juvenile offenders and to determine what their "sentences" will be. These "peer court" programs usually need citizen volunteers to help with coordination and facilitation.

- Serving on county/parish or city/town advisory committees to the local courts, police departments or sheriff's departments.

By working through and with the local courts, Effective Action Teams can build new and better working relationships with local government officials and employees and can gain a more in-depth and professional level of knowledge about local government operations. This in turn enables Effective Action Teams to focus on just the right parts of local government and to work with the people in those departments, agencies, boards, and commissions to get the *leverage* they need to influence local government.

Chapter 6

Putting It All Together: Leverage and Persuasion

Bertrand Russell, in his classic book, *Authority and the Individual* (1949), put it like this:

> "Economic activities on any large scale are determined by those who govern either the state or the large corporations. Even where there is nominally democracy, the part which one citizen can play is usually infinitesimal... As a result of mere size, government becomes increasingly remote from the governed and tends, even in a democracy, to have an independent life of its own."

Was Bertrand Russell correct in his observation? Is our political power as individual citizens so small that there is nothing we can really do to influence our local governments?

When we look at the role of government in our lives today, it is often the case that government, even at the local level, is large, impersonal and remote. Russell's observation is partially correct, in that the size and complexity of government at all levels--federal, state and local--has grown significantly over the last fifty years. As we have learned, however, individual citizens can effectively influence the local governments where they live if they form Effective Action Teams, and if they utilize the methods, "tools," and *leverage points* we have described in this book.

All citizens and citizens' groups have political power and they all have the potential to be effective persuaders who can successfully and effectively use their leverage to influence those who hold the positions of power and authority in local government.

The crucial point, however, is *how* individual citizens or groups use their political power. If they use their political power as well-informed "insiders" who operate with professional attitudes and skills, then they will often achieve success. If they try to influence local government officials and employees with public criticism, anger, yelling, screaming, profanity, uninformed complaints and noisy protests, however, they will almost always fail.

All forms of local government are political systems and they are focused on carrying out their duties and functions as *they believe* the federal and state laws, local ordinances and administrative policies and rules require them to do.

In other words, local government officials and employees generally focus on the processes, procedures and practices of their jobs *first and foremost,* while the needs of local citizens usually fall into a lower priority. The needs and requests of local citizens will be addressed if they appear to fall within the government processes, procedures and practices, but it is up to the local citizens to figure out how to fit their needs and requests into the systems of local government. And, while this is irksome and goes against the grain of our common perceptions of "democracy," it is the reality of local government.

This reality of local government is not new. It has been around for hundreds of years and it is driven by what we call the *traditional inertia* of all organizations. All forms of local government--counties, cities, towns, special districts, school districts and local court systems--operate according to certain traditions. There are certain ways that things are done and have been done for many years, and that is the way it is. And over time the repeated use of certain procedures, practices and processes gathers momentum and becomes a set of forces which has powerful inertia,*i.e. because these bureaucratic forces are in motion, and have been in motion for a long time, they tend to stay in motion, and it is very difficult to redirect or change them.*

The secret to success in changing or redirecting the bureaucratic inertia of local government is found in the use of *leverage and persuasion,* as outlined and described in this book. In summary, here are the critical guidelines that all groups of local citizens must follow in order to be effective and successful in dealing with local government:

1. There is power in numbers. The first step is to gather the members of your group together to form an Effective Action Team. Workers have labor unions, business have business associations like the U.S. Chamber of Commerce, and political groups have political interest groups. They all use professional lobbyists to *leverage and persuade* local government officials and employees. Effective Action Teams do the same thing, but on a smaller scale (see Introduction, Chapter 1 and Chapter 2).

2. Know exactly what you want to accomplish, *why* you want to accomplish it, *how* you think it can be accomplished, and how it will benefit significant members of your local community. Those who try to influence local government for personal, selfish reasons rarely achieve success. Your Effective Action Team needs to put its specific desired outcomes *in writing* and must then develop an *effective project action plan* for how to achieve those desired outcomes. As the old saying goes, if you don't know where you are going, any road will get you there (Introduction, Chapter 1 and Chapter 2).

3. Your Effective Action Team will need knowledgeable and skilled people, strong leaders, funding, information, energy, hard work and time. There are no short cuts. Sustained, focused, *high leverage persuasion* takes time, professional working relationships with local government officials and employees, and tenacity (Introduction, Chapter 1 and Chapter 2).

4. Effective Action Teams must do their homework and learn the key organizational structures, processes and working relationships of local government. Effective Action Teams must focus on *specific leverage points* within the political systems of local government, be it a county, city, town, special district, school district, or the local courts. A *leverage point* is a specific place in the

local government system (like a key manager, committee or agency) where relatively minimum work by local citizens can get maximum results (Introduction).

5.   Learn the *pyramid* of local government bureaucracy, the specialized bureaucratic language and acronyms of local government, and the most important decision-making processes, procedures and timelines (Introduction).

6.   Let pragmatism be your guiding strategy. Learn and follow the written rules of how the game of local government is played and, most importantly, learn and follow the "unwritten rules" (Chapter 1).

7.   *Do your homework.* Learn to love statistics. Dig into government reports, general plans, specific area plans, and a wide range of government documents (Chapter 1).

8.   Establish professional working relationships with local government officials and employees. In addition to learning the "insider language" of local government, your Effective Action Team must build strong working relationships with all of the key decision-makers and bureaucrats (Chapters 1 and 2).

9.   Use the *Toolbox for Dealing Successfully with Local Government.*

   • Choose strong leaders for your Effective Action Team.

   • Recruit skilled and talented people with a wide range of knowledge and skills to join your Effective Action Team. Get the "right people" on the "right bus."

   • Build your team, use dialogue, focus on ideal solutions, and use the *Conditions for Change*, the *Fishbone Diagram,* and the *Transformation Map.*

   • Build your *Project Implementation Plan* then execute it with sustained energy, hard work, tenacity, and professionalism.

- Build professional working relationships with the "gatekeepers" in the local government entity you are working to influence.

- Carefully prepare your research documents, interviews and after-action critique documents.

- Carefully draft, revise and prepare your proposal for submission to the local government entity with whom your group is working.

- Carefully plan, orchestrate and execute your presentation of your proposal at the appropriate local government meeting or meetings.

- Re-visit your professional working relationships with the "gatekeepers" in the local government entity: Follow-up repeatedly and follow-through on any commitments your *Effective Action Team* has made(Chapter 2).

10. If your Effective Action Team is planning to work with one of the specialized forms of local government - the largely "invisible" special districts or school districts, then you must take the time to do even more homework. Dig in and become well informed on the history, organizational structures, processes, procedures and working relationships in the special district or school district which is your target to solve a particular problem or issue (Chapter 3).

11. Learn as much as you can about special interest groups and their agents (lobbyists and other professional consultants). Special interest groups and their agents have a lot of influence and leverage over special districts or school districts and your Effective Action Team must either figure out how to work with them or how to neutralize them (Chapter 3).

12. If your Effective Action Team needs to work with a public school district, take the time to carefully understand the governance processes and key school district decision-makers. Remember that school districts are largely closed, internally-referenced political

systems and they have long-standing internal structural and political conflicts which you must avoid. Keep your focus on what is best for the students and the *Essential Knowledge, Skills, Attitudes and Behaviors* all students must learn, apply and master for success in their adult lives and careers (Chapter 4).

13. After all other options have been tried and exhausted, then, and only then, should your Effective Action Team work to resolve your identified problems or issue with local government in the local court system. Lawsuits are expensive, time consuming and gut-wrenching, and there are lots of procedural traps involved (Chapter 5).

14. If your Effective Action Team does decide to take action through the local court system, please take the time to learn about how the local court systems function, about their traditions and customs, the unique nomenclature used in local courts, and get a skilled, reputable, and experienced attorney to assist you.

As we stated at the outset, dealing effectively with local government is not magic nor is it a mystery. It is all about using the proper *leverage points* in local government organizations and with local government officials and employees, using "insider knowledge," and acting in a professional manner.

Dealing effectively with local government is not easy. It takes a strong group effort, time, energy, information, hard work, money and tenacity. There are no short-cuts and no simple solutions, and those who pursue a strategy of personal attacks on government officials or employees almost always lose. As the old adage goes, "keep your eye on the donut and not on the hole."

Use the power of the Internet to help your Effective Action Team. Recruit some team members who are experts at Internet research. There are tons of resources and valuable, expert information available on the web, but you have to know what you are doing. There are also a few bogus websites just waiting to trap you and take your money.

Remember: Successfully dealing with local government requires high-leverage working relationships, and one of the most effective ways to build such relationships is for your Effective

Action Team to provide local officials with trustworthy, value-added information which they cannot get from anyone else. Once your group is known as a source of expertise and accurate and timely information, your group will have indeed captured a major *leverage point.*

The leaders and employees of any local government like to think of themselves as well-informed, up-to-speed "experts" on the issues of local government. If your Effective Action Team can demonstrate to them that your group can provide them new and better information, then you will become an important source for them in the long term, and your group will acquire an ongoing source of *political power.*

Today knowledge has power. It controls access to opportunity and advancement.

We now accept the fact that learning is a lifelong process of keeping abreast of change. And the most pressing task is to teach people how to learn.

- Dr. Peter Drucker[1]

Appendices

The following documents are valuable "tools" for the work of any local citizens or citizens' groups (hopefully Effective Action Teams) as you seek success in working with local government.

Conditions for Change™©

The *Conditions for Change*™© concept and "tool" was developed by our friend and colleague Don Prentice. The use of this tool will save any citizen or citizens' group a lot of time, money and effort. When your group is considering any problem, issue or project, please use it to see if all of the *Conditions for Change*™ are present and in place. If they are not, then you will need to analyze what it would take to get them in place. Getting them in place may prove to be reasonable, practical and possible. If getting them in place seems to be impractical, unreasonable, too difficult or too costly in terms of time, energy and money, then stop, rethink it, and come at it from a different direction or abandon it. You will save yourself a lot of frustration and avoid failure.

The *Conditions for Change*™© were created by Don Prentice with assistance from Alec I. Ostrom and is trademarked and copyrighted by Don Prentice and Alec I. Ostrom and may not be used or reproduced without prior written permission. The readers of *Leverage Points – A Universal Guide for Success in Dealing with Local Government* are welcome to use the *Conditions for Change*™© "tool" as long as they do not reproduce it for sale. This permission is granted as a limited use authorization and it is only available to those who have purchased our book.

Conditions for Change ™

Introduction: Before starting on any project to address or resolve a serious, substantive and/or complex problem or issue, it is always best to first consider the overall *Conditions for Change*™©. Many people assume that because they have identified what they believe to be a workable solution or resolution to a problem or issue that everyone else will go along with what they are proposing to do. In most organizations, however--local government institutions, businesses, school districts and community organizations--there is a strong *existing organizational culture* that is usually resistant to any sort of proposed change or transformation.

The *people* in any organization or situation usually determine the success of any proposed change. Therefore, the people involved must:

UNDERSTAND THE PROPOSED CHANGE

People must understand the purpose, rationale, benefits, and implications of any proposed change. People must be fully informed participants in the proposed change process.

HAVE ADEQUATE AND PROPER RESOURCES

Necessary resources must be available: Information, time, energy, funding, expertise, training, equipment, policies, etc.

SEE THE CHANGE AS IN THEIR OWN SELF INTEREST

People must see the proposed change as in their own self interest, as they define that interest. Threats of negative consequences may get the appearance of compliance, but they will not get commitment and energy.

COLLABORATE TO CREATE THE PROPOSED CHANGE

If people are affected by a proposed change, they must be involved in creating it. Imposing change on people involved as passive agents, or forcing change with political power is a proven formula for generating resistance and, in most cases, ultimate failure.

When all four Conditions of Change™© are present they will generate:
STRONG PEOPLE COMMITMENT

AND

STRONG MOBILIZED PEOPLE ENERGY

Without these, you will get pro forma compliance, resistance, and even sabotage.

ALL FOUR of these *Conditions for Change*™ must be present in order for any proposed transformation to have a reasonable chance of success. Checking the presence of these *Conditions for Change*™ will help you prevent or resolve costly problems, mistakes and time delays with proposed change initiatives.

Transformation Map™©

Please note that the *Transformation Map*™© concept and document were created by Don Prentice with assistance from Alec I. Ostrom and that the *Transformation Map*™© is trademarked and copyrighted by Don Prentice and Alec I. Ostrom and may not be used or reproduced without prior written permission. The readers of *Leverage Points – A Universal Guide for Success in Dealing with Local Government* are welcome to use the *Transformation Map*™© "tool" as long as they do not reproduce it for sale. This permission is granted as a limited use authorization and it is only available to those who have purchased our book.

Transformation Map™

Before starting on any project to address a serious, substantive or complex issue, it is always best to first construct a *Transformation Map*™ to pre-plan your action project. Leaping into action always feels good at first but without a *Transformation Map*™ initial enthusiasms and hard work often dissolve into frustration and failure because unforeseen obstacles emerge and there is no plan or resources to address them.

Failing to plan is planning to fail, and it is not *what you think of* that destroys an action project but *what you **don't** think of.* Taking the time to complete the *Transformation Map*™ pre-planning process on the *front end* of any action project will produce significantly greater chances for success.

What is a *Transformation Map*™?

A *Transformation Map*™ is just what its title implies – it is a "map" that guides us and helps us to find our way through any

change or transformation process. This has five essential components:

- A clear understanding and description of the problem to be solved or the issue to be resolved.

- A detailed description of the *desired outcomes* of the optimum solution or resolution to the identified problem or issue.

- A detailed description of the *necessary and sufficient conditions* that must be in place in order to achieve or accomplish the desired outcomes of the optimum solution or resolution.

- A detailed description of the *existing conditions* which are present in the working context for the identified problem or issue.

- A detailed description of the specific *action steps and tasks* that need to be integrated into a full Project Implementation Plan.

Let's start with an example of a typical kind of change. Let's say that in a given organization--a business, school district, community organization or some department or agency of local government--there is a program to train the employees to improve their computer skills. We discover that a majority of the employees are having trouble with the training program and there are many complaints about the training manuals, which are hard to read and very confusing.

As a result, the team of trainers meets and quickly decides to find and purchase a new set of training manuals. They gather up several sample manuals from different training companies, and do some rapid research on the Internet to find which manuals are recommended and widely-used. They recommend their selection to the upper-level managers of the organization, who review their recommendation and authorize the funding to purchase the new manuals.

The trainers start using the new manuals in the computer-training program only to discover that they themselves need more time to learn how to use the new manuals. They also discover that several of the employees find the *new* training manuals hard to read and still confusing.

As time goes on, the trainers have more conversations with the employees and they discover that the real issue is that the contents of the training manuals (old and new) do not match the kinds of computer work the employees are doing. They are having a hard time transferring the general computer knowledge from the manuals to their specific uses of computers in their jobs.

Leaping into action and purchasing new training manuals felt good, and seemed to be the right thing to do but, as we now know, this change did not work out very well. It cost a good deal of time, money and effort, to say nothing of the employees' frustration, with very little to show in positive results.

Using a *Transformation Map*™ will help to eliminate most (if not all) of these kinds of obstacles with any transformation process.

How to Use the *Transformation Map*™ process – step by step:

The *Transformation Map*™ process involves a number of steps which are listed below. These steps may seem to be unfamiliar and the entire process may seem confusing and time-consuming at first but, with practice, the process will become easier and faster. Whenever we make any change, we actually perform these steps already. In most cases, we just don't realize we are doing them, which is why some of the steps are often assumed, overlooked, or done poorly.

The *Transformation Map*™ pre-planning process actually *saves* time, energy, money and work, and it helps to prevent frustration and failure. As noted in the computer training example above, the first action didn't take much time but, the failure to adequately understand the true issues and problems wasted time, effort and money AND the trainers team had to start all over again. The wasted resources in that example cost far more than the time it takes to create a *Transformation Map*™ on the front end of the transformation process.

The *Transformation Map*™ pre-planning process includes the following steps:

1.   **Identify and describe the problem(s) or issue(s) to be addressed.**

In almost all change or transformation processes, we work to solve a problem or to resolve some issue. The first step, therefore, is to *describe the problem or issue in writing, with as much detail as possible.* Here are some questions that may be helpful in describing the issue:

- What specific indicators or symptoms are we seeing or feeling that tell us that there is a problem? Are people experiencing pain, frustration, or obstacles that seem difficult to overcome?

- Is the organization unable to deliver its normal products or services?

- Is the organization experiencing financial losses, increased costs difficulties in its operations or working relationships?

- Are the "customers" or "clients" of the organization frustrated and unhappy?

- If we look deeply and get beyond the indicators or symptoms of the trouble, what is the *real core problem or issue?* What is the *root cause* of the problems or issues that everyone is experiencing?

2.   **Identify the desired outcomes that will ideally solve the problem or resolve the issue.**

There are usually a number of potential solutions to an issue; the trick is to find and use the *optimum* one. What does the term *optimum* mean in this situation? It means that the solution to a problem or the resolution of an issue is achieved in the immediate short term *and* also provides the means to sustain the solution well into the future.

Finding the *optimum* resolution is not easy but the best place to start is to identify the *desired outcomes* that would ideally be part of the solution. A *desired outcome* is simply a stated description of what people would like to occur or establish after the problem is solved.

Here are some helpful guidelines for identifying the *desired outcomes* you would like to achieve or accomplish:

- Brainstorm a list of as many *desired outcomes* as you would like to have in place after you resolve the issue at hand. List everything you can think of no matter how absurd it may seem.

- When you are brainstorming your desired outcomes list, assume that you have no limitations of any kind: no limits on time, money, human resources, policies, laws, equipment, infrastructure, etc. This is important because some critical desired outcomes may be left out if you assume that you can't even try to accomplish them because of some perceived constraints or obstacles that have not been fully explored.

- As you list and describe *each* desired outcome, try to use as much detail as possible and leave nothing out.

- As you list *each* desired outcome, try to describe it in ways that can be measured--i.e. when a particular desired outcome is reached, how will you know it, and that it is complete, and that it is working the way you would like it to work?

- Don't worry about sequencing your *desired outcomes* or putting them in any sort of priority at this point; just get them down and describe each one in excruciating detail.

3. **For each desired outcome that you identified, list and describe the necessary and sufficient conditions which must exist in order for each particular desired outcome to be achieved or completed:**

A *condition* is anything that is required to make each desired outcome a reality. Conditions include such things as time, money, information, expertise, training, planning, processes, equipment, infrastructure, assessment or evaluation processes, feed-forward processes, feedback processes, working relationships between employees and management, relationships with customers or clients or vendors, transportation, supply chain components, computer networks, and so on.

A *necessary condition* is one that absolutely must be in place; if not, then the particular desired outcome simply cannot be accomplished. In the computer training example, one of the *necessary conditions* (which was missing) was a deep understanding of how the computer training would be used by the employees in their individual jobs in the organization.

A *sufficient condition* is one that is in place *and* at a level of quality and/or quantity that is needed to reasonably achieve success.

Here are some guidelines which may be helpful in identifying and describing the *necessary and sufficient conditions* which must be in place to achieve or accomplish your identified desired outcomes:

- For each desired outcome brainstorm as many statements of *necessary and sufficient conditions* as you can. Again, don't put any pre-supposed constraints on your deliberations and list everything you can imagine, even if it seems absurd.

- If you are working on desired outcomes related to an optimum solution that is difficult or complex, start with a simple practice problem or issue.

  For example: *Solution:* The menu in the organization's cafeteria or lunch room will have a variety of soups, salads, vegetarian dishes, healthy meat/fish/chicken dishes, breads, vegetable side dishes, and a diverse offering of choices from different ethnic cultures.

  What are the *necessary and sufficient conditions* that must be in place in order to achieve this particular cafeteria or lunch room menu (*desired outcome*)?

  (1) "Variety" will need to be defined in detail.

(2) The term "vegetarian" will need to be defined in detail.

(3) "Healthy" needs to be defined in detail.

(4) The descriptor "different ethnic cultures" needs to be defined in detail.

(5) The available budget to support the cafeteria menu will need to be researched, and any additional funds to support the new menu will have to be identified and secured.

(6) The employees and managers will need to be surveyed, to see what specific types of dishes they want included in the menu.

(7) The capability and expertise of the kitchen chef, cooks and staff will have to be explored to see if they can produce the desired menu, or if they need additional training.

We won't list all of the *necessary and sufficient conditions* in this simple example, but you get the idea.

- Be sure to go beyond the typical *necessary and sufficient conditions* of time, money, equipment, training, etc. In achieving or accomplishing most desired outcomes (especially those that are part of a complex solution or resolution) one of the critical *necessary and sufficient conditions* is **relevant, complete and timely information.**

- Also, be sure to deeply explore working relationships, political realities (such as laws, regulations, policies, etc. as well as informal ones, like traditions and entrenched practices and beliefs) and the whole area of a **strong consensus agreement** for moving forward with a particular Project Implementation Plan.

- Take the time to examine assumptions and beliefs; assume nothing, take nothing for granted, and overlook nothing. Leave no stone unturned when it comes to *necessary and sufficient conditions.*

4. **For each desired outcome that you have identified, list and describe the existing conditions that are already in place.**

Problems or issues which need to be addressed do not exist in a vacuum. They usually emerge in a particular organizational working context. Our computer training example above could and usually does exist in most organizations, and the point here is that, when we are trying to solve problems or resolve issues, we need to pay attention to the *organizational context* in which they are occurring.

This fourth step in the *Transformation Map™* pre-planning process is the step that is most often ignored when people are trying to solve a problem or resolve an issue. We human beings get so used to the place where we work (the *organizational context*) that we just automatically *assume* that certain processes or working relationships are already in place, so we do not need to worry about them in trying to resolve issues. These conditions are sort of like a nice radio station playing soft music in the background, so we gloss right over them in our thinking and planning, but to our peril.

For each desired outcome you have described, please list the *existing conditions* that are already in place and that are in any way related to finding and implementing the *optimum* solution and desired outcomes you are seeking.

In our computer training example, there were several *existing conditions* that the trainers ignored or overlooked as they acted quickly to solve problems. Here are a few of them:

- They recognized and listened to the complaints from the employees about the existing training manuals, but they did not have any meaningful dialogue with the employees about why the manuals were hard to read and use. Had they done so, they would have discovered the real problem which was that the general content in the training manuals was hard for the employees to apply to their specific job tasks.

- The computer training program was already in place, so it obviously had a specific purpose and objectives, but the trainers assumed that these elements were okay and did not take the time to re-examine them or discuss them with the employees.

- The trainers assumed that the training methods they were using were also sufficient. Again, they did not re-examine these *existing conditions* nor did they discuss them with the employees.

- The trainers assumed that the employees found the computer training program to be useful and meaningful relative to their specific jobs in the organization, as the employees only complained about the manuals. Maybe the entire training program needed to be examined and re-evaluated before doing anything specific like buying new manuals.

- And of course, there are the typical *existing conditions:* the funding of the computer training program, the time and space, the scheduling of the training, the existing number of trainers and their levels of expertise in computers and in teaching, the policies authorizing the training program, and the employee performance assessment processes to determine if the they complete the computer training program in proper fashion.

We will stop here with the examples of *existing conditions,* but you can see that there are many others that might be listed for this particular example.

It is absolutely critical to list and describe in painful detail all of the *existing conditions* that you can. Please examine all assumptions and leave no stone unturned in completing this fourth step in the *Transformation Map™* pre-planning process. Remember, it is what you *don't* think of which will come back later to bite you.

5. **The fifth and last step in the Transformation Map™ pre-planning process is to compare and contrast your list of necessary and sufficient conditions with your list of existing conditions to identify any differences or "gaps" between the two lists, and then to use this information to develop specific action items (or sets of action items) that are needed to put the proper conditions in place to achieve your desired outcomes and to put your optimum solution or resolution in place.**

In most cases, especially those with difficult, challenging or complex issues and equally challenging solutions, the *necessary and sufficient conditions* list will usually far outnumber the *existing conditions* list. This will enable you to identify those new *necessary and sufficient conditions* that you will need to establish.

Also, as you compare and contrast the two lists of conditions, you may discover some of the *existing conditions* need to be repaired, restructured, revised or clarified and improved.

Once you have identified the new *necessary and sufficient conditions* that you need to put in place and any *existing conditions* that you need to revise, you then have all the components you need to put together a solid, workable and practical *Project Implementation Plan* or PIP.

* * * * * * * *

On the following page there is a simplified example of a Project Implementation Plan Form to get you started. Project Implementation Plans can become complex and large but, in the beginning, it is best to keep your PIP simple, focused and easy to understand. You can always add to it or modify it later as you get into the actual implementation process.

Now that you have a *Transformation Map™*, all you need is to plug the information into the PIP Form. The PIP Form here is just an example. You may expand the boxes to any size you need. A typical PIP will usually have several pages.

Again, it is usually best to take a simple problem (like the cafeteria menu example), complete the *Transformation Map*™ pre-planning process as a practice run, and then complete a draft PIP.

Project Implementation Plan (PIP) Simplified Form: | Page__of___

Project Title: _____Draft # _____ Date:_____

Identify and describe the details of the problem to be solved or the issue to be resolved:
5.
6.
7.
8.

Describe the details of the Desired Outcomes that will make up the Optimum solution or resolution:

5.

6.

7.

8.

Necessary and Sufficient Conditions or Revised and Improved Existing Conditions to achieve/complete the Desired Outcomes:

5.

6.

7.

8.

Action Set Number_____to put the N & S and/or Revised/Improved Existing Conditions in place and the tasks related thereto:

Action Steps:

5.

6.

7.

8.

Tasks	Dependencies	Resources	Metrics	Persons Responsible	Deadlines
1. Describe required work	Order of tasks	Time, funds, Information, Training, Equipment, Software, Expertise, Processes Etc.	How progress will be assessed in stages or phases and evaluated at project end	List names	List dates

2. Describe each task completely including processes, actions, specific work, working relationships, etc.

3. Don't assume anything; describe what needs to be done even if it seems obvious.

4. The initial tasks must put the necessary and sufficient conditions in place to achieve other tasks and to achieve or complete the desired outcomes.

Sample Interview Guidelines

When someone from your citizens' group (Effective Action Team) sets up an appointment to interview a local government official, manager or employee, please keep in mind the following objectives:

- Your group is working on getting to know the "gatekeepers" in the local government--the people who make the decisions and who have the vital information you need.

- Your group is working on building professional relationships with the "gatekeepers." You want these people to help you and to be your allies.

Guidelines for your meeting and interview or conversation with any local government official, manager or employee:

1. Introduce yourself and all of the people in your group. Interviews or meetings are best with only one or two people. Local government officials usually don't like to meet with larger groups of people in private. Remember to be courteous and professional at all times.

2. Provide the person with a brief one-page document that explains what you are working on and why, then briefly review it with them. Focus on no more than one or two key points.

3. Explain that you are seeking their help, guidance and information. Emphasize that you are not there to complain or to criticize anyone. If, during the conversation, the person gets defensive, angry or upset, don't overreact. Remain calm and listen to what they are saying, even if it is being said in a gruff or angry way.

4. Ask the person to briefly explain what he or she does in local government, and to give you some background information on his or her areas of responsibility.

5. Ask the person to help you better understand the *problem or issue* you are working on. For example: "We are very concerned about crime in our neighborhood. We need to

know how we should document, illustrate and explain the criminal acts we are seeing in our neighborhood. How should we do that? What guidelines should we follow? What information do we need to have?"

Also, have some specific questions about your *problem or issue* prepared in advance and work them into the conversation.

6.   Ask the person for any historical or background information they might be able to give you on your *problem or issue.*

7.   Ask for their suggestions or recommendations on how your group should research and prepare potential solutions to your issue. If the person asks you what solution ideas you have in mind, be prepared to give them a brief, one-page handout that describes the specific solutions you are *tentatively considering.* Make it clear that you and your group are just seeking information, guidance and help.

8.   As the discussion proceeds, try to keep it open-ended. Ask the person for their thoughts and ideas. Ask them for suggestions or recommendations, and to provide some questions that your group may need to address or research.

9.   Ask for any documents or handouts that he or she may have that might be helpful. Ask the person that, if your group prepares a specific proposal, is there a particular proposal form or format that you should follow, or existing documents that would help you in formulating a proposal.

10.   As the discussion nears its end, ask the person for their specific ideas as your "next steps."

11.   Be very cognizant of their time. If the interview is scheduled for 15 minutes or 30 minutes, be sure to end a bit early, and never push the person beyond the scheduled time. Also, if the person gets interrupted during your conversation or must end the conversation early, don't get angry or upset. Tell the person that you understand and that you will work with her or him to reschedule an appointment at a later time.

Also, if your group feels that you did not get all of the information you needed, ask if it would be okay to schedule a follow-up appointment.

12. Be sure to thank the person for their time, information and assistance. Shake hands, smile and depart in a prompt and orderly manner. Never leave in an angry huff or in any manner which is disrespectful. Keep your cool and always be courteous and civil.

13. If the government official, manager and/or employee has a secretary or administrative assistant, be sure to introduce yourself to that person and ask for his or her telephone number in case you need to schedule any future meetings and to facilitate any future contacts.

14. Always send the local government official, manager or employee a written thank-you note within two days, via the U.S. mail.

After Action Critique

Any time your group meets with a local government official, manager or employee, or any time your group participates in or merely attends a local government meeting or event, it always pays dividends to get your group together as soon as possible after the meeting to do an *After Action Critique.*

The purpose and objectives of an *After Action Critique* are as follows:

*   To compare notes from everyone in your group who was in attendance or participated. You will discover that different people in your group will hear or observe different things, or will have different impressions or feelings about the event, and you need to get all of those things recorded and documented before they are forgotten.

*   To do a self-examination of the performance of the members of your group who participated.

- To identify what you learned from the interview, meeting or event, and to quickly jot down any ideas or questions about what you learned.

- To identify what you did *not learn* from the interview, meeting or event, and what additional questions need to be asked or research needs to be done.

- To clarify the group's "next steps" or specific action items in the process.

Some sample questions that need to be raised in an *After Action Critique:*

1. [To each person] What impressions did you have of today's interview with [name], or today's meeting, or today's event?

2. [To each person] What really stood out for you about today's interview, meeting or event?

3. [To each person] What did we learn from today's interview, meeting or event? What did we learn that will really help us to move forward with our project?

4. [To each person] What was missing from today's interview, meeting or event? What were the local government officials, managers and/or employees *not* saying? What information were they withholding, if any? What things did they seem reluctant to talk about? What additional questions do we need to ask them? What additional information do we need?

5. What additional research do we need to do, based on what we learned today?

6. What are some "next steps" or action items we need to act on based on what we learned today?

7. How did we do today? What did we need to differently or better? Where did we really succeed today? Where did we really mess up today? And, what did we learn from our successes and/or our mistakes?

How to prepare and write a high quality proposal

When your group is ready to prepare and deliver a proposal package to a particular branch of local government, you will need to find out what the specific requirements are for making a proposal and what format must be followed in preparing the document(s). Contact one of the "gatekeepers" in your local government to get this information.

We recommend that you visit the following websites to get more information on preparing project proposals for any local government:

- The Appalachian Regional Commission website has an excellent outline and clear description for how to prepare proposals, at:

  http://www.arc.gov/funding/HowtoWriteaGrant Proposal.asp.

- The ARC website outline refers to the guidelines for how to prepare a proposal to obtain a grant, but the guidelines will work for the preparation of any proposal.

- There is a good sample of how to prepare a proposal, written by Eric Rinehart and Barbara Bouie-Scott, entitled *The Basic Steps in Planning and Writing A Successful Grant Application* and it can be found at:

  http://www.commerce.state.il.us/NR/rdonlyres/EC10F8 34-50A0-4CB0-8121- B6185951F91D/0/ProposalWriting2003.pdf.

  Once again, these guidelines are for writing a grant application, but they are valid and useful for developing and writing any kind of proposal.

- The McMaster University Office of Research Services has a good listing of the components of a good proposal:

http://www.mcmaster.ca/ors/guide/successful_proposal.htm.

McMaster University also has more information on writing proposals at:

http://www.mcmaster.ca/ors/guide/guide_proposal.htm.

- Here is a good interactive guide for writing funding proposals, written by Dr. S. Joseph Levine of Michigan State University:

http://www.learnerassociates.net/proposal/.

These guidelines pertain to writing proposals to obtain funding, but they are also useful for developing any proposal.

- The website ProposalWriter.com also has some good samples of well-prepared and well-written government proposals:

http://www.proposalwriter.com/grantsamples.html.

Glossary

For citizens and Effective Action Teams to achieve success with local government they must learn the "insider" language or nomenclature used by local government. This glossary is intended to provide you with some of the words, terms, acronyms and jargon frequently used by those in local government.

These definitions are described within the context of the methods, "tools," and *leverage points* we have described and explained in this book.

Our glossary is selective and is not intended to be a comprehensive listing of governmental or political terminology. Many of the terms used in local government have already been defined in each chapter of our book, so they are not all repeated here. It would be helpful for readers to dig into the specific terms used by the local governments where they live, as "local usage" varies.

Leverage Points –

A Universal Guide for Success in Dealing with Local Government

INTRODUCTION

Bureaucracy: A bureaucracy is defined as [1] a: a body of non-elective government officials, or b: an administrative policy-making group; [2]: government characterized by specialization of functions, adherence to fixed rules, and a hierarchy of authority; [3]: a system of administration marked by officialism, red tape, and proliferation. From the Merriam-Webster Dictionary online: http://www.merriam-webster.com/dictionary/bureaucracy.

Political System: A political system is defined as the set of formal legal institutions that constitute a "government" or a "state." This is the definition adopted by many studies of the legal or constitutional arrangements of advanced political orders. More broadly defined, however, the term comprehends actual as well as prescribed forms of political behavior, not only the legal organization of the state but also the reality of how the state functions. From the *Encyclopedia Britannica* online: http://www.britannica.com/EBchecked/topic/467746/political-system.

Political Power: *The ability to influence or control the thoughts and actions of other people.* If you can influence at least one other person then, you have some measure of *political power.* And while there are many historical examples of *political power* wielded by military force or police action or totalitarian governments, most of the time *political power* comes from the control of the flow of *information.* Local officials use their ability to control information to keep themselves in power. They do it in two ways: [1] By *withholding* or *restricting* the flow of information--as citizens who don't know about something can't act on it, and [2] By *controlling what kind of information is released to the public, as well as how and when it is released.* Again, if local citizens don't find out about some critical information until *after* local government officials have acted on it, there is little that they can do about it. The *completeness, truthfulness and quality of the information* released by local government officials allows them to use their "insider" positions of political power to control what is going on.

Professional Politician: A person experienced in the art or science of government; one actively engaged in conducting the business of government. Someone who engages in conducting the business of government as his or her career. Professional politicians are usually the elected officials who serve on local government city councils, county boards of supervisors, county commissions, parishes (the governing bodies in Louisiana), town councils, school boards, and/or the boards or commissions or "authorities" of special (purpose) districts. Professional politicians usually seek to hold some sort of political office at all times and they continually seek to be elected, re-elected or appointed.

In order to deal successfully with your local government, citizens and citizens' groups will need to become politicians themselves. The difference is that they are *amateur* politicians, especially in the beginning stages of their work on a particular problem or issue. The secrets to success for *amateur* politicians can be boiled down to two elements:

- Citizens and citizens' groups, as *amateur* politicians, need to learn the "insider" language, the "insider" processes, and the "insider" people and working relationships of local government.

- Citizens and citizens' groups, as *amateur* politicians, need to study the professional politicians very closely: How they think, how they make decisions, how they perceive certain problems or issues, how they work with other people inside and outside of government, and what their personal and professional preferences and personalities are like.

1. **Political System:** All forms of local government--cities, towns, counties, parishes, special districts, school districts, local courts, etc.--are *political systems.* They are organizations established and operated to carry out the business of government in some fashion. They have the organizational capacity to solicit and accept informational *input* from citizens, citizens' groups, interest groups, political parties, businesses, community organizations including churches, etc. They have the organizational capacity and authority to create specific *outputs* such as policies, ordinances, regulations, rules, bureaucratic administrative decisions, court rulings, court orders, etc.

    All local governments are *political systems* and the key to understanding them is to focus on the interdependencies and connections between their component functions and their officials, managers and employees. *Political systems* are just like the human body: to understand them and how they function, citizens must learn about the various *parts* of local government, but more importantly *how all of those parts connect to each other and how they work together.*

2.   **Leverage Points:** We chose to use the title *Leverage Points* for this book because local citizens need to understand that the key to success in dealing with any local government is to identify the *leverage points* in the organization or system, and to use those *leverage points* to influence local government officials, managers or employees.

We all know the power of a fulcrum and a lever. When you get a flat tire and you use a "jack" to lift up your car to change a flat tire, you are using a fulcrum (the jack) and a lever (the jack handle). When you are moving a big rock, you use a pry bar with something underneath it to get the "leverage" you need. The same thing is true with local government. The key is knowing *where* to place your "pry bar" so that the information and influence you have gets the *maximum intended effect,* i.e., you cause the local government to move, or to take action to do what you would like it to do.

Our friend and colleague Don Prentice developed the idea of *leverage points* after working with all sorts of organizational systems and his notion is to focus on the places in any organization where two or more processes or functions connect. When a citizens' group is able to influence one of these connection points or *leverage points* then there is a powerful ripple effect throughout the whole organization of any local government.

3.   **Requirements:** Most of us already know about requirements. Let's look at an example: In order to vote in local government elections, all citizens must first meet some specific *requirements*: They must be 18 years of age, a legal resident in the community (usually a town, city and/or county and/or state), and they have to register to vote by a certain deadline.

In negotiating successfully with local governments, some start with idealistic *ideas* or *goals* that they want to accomplish (like having more and better local parks and recreational areas), but they often fail because they do not take the time to seek out, identify, and carefully understand all of the *requirements* that must be met in order to achieve their goals.

Between any two people or organizations, in order to accomplish a specific task or process or project, the *requirements must be [a] clear, exact and valid; [b] mutually understood; and [c] mutually agreed upon.*

4. **Administrative Law(s):** Town councils, city councils, county/parish boards of supervisors, special district boards or commissions, school district boards of education, and so forth, operate under federal and state laws which give them the authority to make local laws. These local laws are usually called *ordinances, policies or regulations.*

For example, let's say a city council passes an ordinance that all new single family homes built within the city limits must utilize some forms of alternative energy and conserve energy use, such as solar panels, heavier layers of insulation, dual-pane windows, water flow restrictors, etc. And the ordinance also says that any single family homes build *before* 2010 must establish and implement a five-year plan to bring themselves into compliance with the new ordinance. This would require the development and implementation of a whole new set of fairly complex regulations, which then have to be enforced. The development of those regulations and enforcement is *administrative law.*

This means that a department in a local government is empowered under a local ordinance, policy or regulation, to create the specific rules and requirements local citizens must follow to meet the new law. It also means that that same department will be empowered to *interpret and implement* the new regulations on a case-by-case basis. So, when a building contractor files an application for a building permit to build a new home, that contractor must follow the new ordinance and all of the new regulations to enforce it.

The formal definition of Administrative Law is as follows: *Administrative Law is defined as "the body of law governing administrative agencies". It is broken down to include administrative rules, regulations and procedures for government agencies and bodies; the scope of agency authority, in particular individual privacy; and enforcement powers of agencies.* This formal definition is quoted on the website of Coover and Barr, Attorneys at Law: http://www.cooverbarr.com/faqs.html#administrative. In simpler terms, administrative law consists of the rules, regulations and procedures developed by local government departments, agencies, commissions, etc. to carry out federal laws, state laws, and local ordinances or policies. Administrative law is *delegated law* because the authority of those who work in local government bureaucracies is given to them by those in higher positions of power: county, borough or parish supervisors, city council members, special district boards or commissions, local court judges, etc.

Chapter 1: Pragmatism
A Strategy for Dealing Effectively with Local Government

1. **Charters:** Almost all of the 50 states have provisions in their state constitutions which describe the rules and procedures for the establishment of county or parish governments, incorporated city governments, town governments, special district governments, school districts, etc. We have selected the following sections from the Constitution of the State of California which describe exactly what *local government charters* must include and how they are established:

    CALIFORNIA CONSTITUTION

    ARTICLE 11 LOCAL GOVERNMENT

    SEC. 3. (a) For its own government, a county or city may adopt a charter by majority vote of its electors voting on the question. The charter is effective when filed with the Secretary of State. A charter may be amended, revised, or repealed in the same manner. A charter, amendment, revision, or repeal thereof shall be published in the official state statutes. County charters adopted pursuant to this section shall supersede any existing charter and all laws inconsistent therewith. The provisions of a charter are the law of the State and have the force and effect of legislative enactments.

(b) The governing body or charter commission of a county or city may propose a charter or revision. Amendment or repeal may be proposed by initiative or by the governing body.

(c) An election to determine whether to draft or revise a charter and elect a charter commission may be required by initiative or by the governing body.

(d) If provisions of 2 or more measures approved at the same election conflict, those of the measure receiving the highest affirmative vote shall prevail.

CALIFORNIA CONSTITUTION
ARTICLE 11 LOCAL GOVERNMENT

SEC. 4. County charters shall provide for:

(a) A governing body of 5 or more members, elected (1) by district or, (2) at large, or (3) at large, with a requirement that they reside in a district. Charter counties are subject to statutes that relate to apportioning population of governing body districts.

(b) The compensation, terms, and removal of members of the governing body. If a county charter provides for the Legislature to prescribe the salary of the governing body, such compensation shall be prescribed by the governing body by ordinance.

(c) An elected sheriff, an elected district attorney, an elected assessor, other officers, their election or appointment, compensation, terms and removal.

(d) The performance of functions required by statute.

(e) The powers and duties of governing bodies and all other county officers, and for consolidation and segregation of county officers, and for the manner of filling all vacancies occurring therein.

(f) The fixing and regulation by governing bodies, by ordinance, of the appointment and number of assistants, deputies, clerks, attaches, and other persons to be employed, and for the prescribing and regulating by such bodies of the powers, duties, qualifications, and compensation of such persons, the times at which, and terms for which they shall be appointed, and the manner of their appointment and removal.

(g) Whenever any county has framed and adopted a charter, and the same shall have been approved by the Legislature as herein provided, the general laws adopted by the Legislature in pursuance of Section 1(b) of this article, shall, as to such county, be superseded by said charter as to matters for which, under this section it is competent to make provision in such charter, and for which provision is made therein, except as herein otherwise expressly provided.

(h) Charter counties shall have all the powers that are provided by this Constitution or by statute for counties.

2. **Purpose(s) and Desired Outcomes:** When local citizens or citizens' groups set out to address an issue or to solve some problem with local government, they often get confused in how they define, document and utilize their specific *purposes* and *desired outcomes.* To achieve success in dealing with local government, citizens' groups should take whatever time they need to take at the beginning (or on the front end) of their work to clearly define a *purpose or purposes* for what they are doing and the *specific desired outcomes* they would like to accomplish. Their *purpose(s) and desired outcomes* need to be clearly defined, described and written out in detail.

In defining and describing the *purpose(s)* of what your citizens' group is doing, we suggest the following simple introductory phrase:

The purpose (or purposes) of our project is to:_____.

Fill in the "blank" with a clear, direct statement or statements of your purpose. Example: "The purpose of our project is to significantly reduce crime in our city."

Then write in specific detail what your **desired outcomes** are and how they will enable your group to achieve or accomplish its purpose. *Desired outcomes* must be specific, detailed and *measureable*. For example, in order to reduce crime in our city, *one* of our *desired outcomes* is to increase the number of police on patrol from six (6) two-person patrol cars per shift (overlapping time segments of eight hours) to eight (8) two-person patrol cars per shift.

This is a well-stated *desired outcome* because it describes exactly what your citizens' group wants to achieve (two more two-person patrol cars per shift), it is detailed, and it is measureable. If your citizens' group can convince the city council to approve your request, then this *desired outcome* can be measured: Did you get two more two-person patrol cars per shift or not? The answers must be clear and specific: Yes, we got two more two-person patrol cars per shift, OR we got one more two-person patrol car per shift, OR we got one more two-person patrol car but only for the night shift, OR we did not get any increase in two-person patrol cars for any shift, etc.

Also, by stating your *desired outcomes* in specific detail and in ways that are measureable, you will be able to identify and describe the specific *necessary and sufficient conditions* which must be put in place to achieve or accomplish each *desired outcome*.

An example of a poorly stated *desired outcome* would be: "Our group wants increased police patrols in our neighborhood." What does "increased" mean? What does "our neighborhood" mean? What does "police patrols" mean? This *desired outcome* statement is too general.

3.   **Professional Working Relationships:** Perhaps the best way to think about the working relationships you need to establish with local government officials, managers and/or employees is to think about them as you would other highly valued and expert people in your life: Your doctor, your attorney, your priest/pastor/minister/rabbi/imam, your dentist, your veterinarian, etc.

Too often, citizens think of local government officials, managers and/or employees as their "public servants," or as people who are not necessarily "experts" in the products or services they deliver. On TV talk shows, government officials are often depicted as irresponsible, unethical, or incompetent, and "government" at any level is depicted as "just a bunch of bureaucrats who screw things up." Also, we often hear the phrase, "Hey, I'm a taxpayer, those guys in the government work for me."

The reality is that we have a representative form of democracy which enables us as citizens and voters to elect local government officials: members of a town council, city council, county board of supervisors, special district board or commission members, school board members, etc. These elected officials, in turn, are responsible for hiring managers to operate the various operational departments or functions of local government, and the managers in turn hire the employees who work for them. All of these folks are responsible for delivering high quality, timely, competent, efficient and effective government services, but they are not "servants;" they are either elected officials or employed or appointed managers or employees.

To be successful in dealing with all local government officials, managers and employees, citizens and citizens' groups need to build civil, courteous, honest, and friendly working relationships with these people, who should be treated just like any other professional persons that we might go to for services or that any of us might employ. That doesn't mean that we can't disagree with them or notify them if they are acting improperly, but it does mean that we need to learn to work with them, to get to know them, and to treat them just like any other group of professionals.

4. **Context (in dealing with statistics or data reports):** Local government officials, managers and employees seem to live and die with numbers. It is very important, therefore, for citizens and citizens' groups to become familiar with the statistical reports and data reports that local governments use.

It is also important for citizens and groups to seek out the information they will need to fully understand the *context* for these statistical and data reports. The *context* means that <u>set of conditions from which</u> the statistics or data were derived or generated AND that <u>set of conditions in which</u> the statistics or data will be used. Here are some useful examples of these "conditions":

Conditions from which the statistics or data were derived or generated:

- Reports by professional researchers, accountants, supervisors, state or federal agencies or departments, etc. Check out the credentials of the report writers and those who prepared the numbers.

- Local surveys of residents in a region, community or neighborhood. Look carefully at how the surveys were conducted and who did the surveys.

- Annual reports by government officials, managers or employees. Look carefully at who did the research, what methodologies they used, what guidelines they used, and also check out who actually prepared these annual reports.

- Other required government reports or research studies such as Environmental Impact Reports, Negative Declaration Reports, Evaluation Reports, Accreditation Reports, etc.

- On all of these kinds of reports, check the *time frame* of when the report was prepared (is the information current and up to date?), and the range and depth of the statistics or data that is used. In a community of 50,000 people, a report or survey doesn't mean much if it only comes from 50 people.

Conditions in which the statistics or data will be used:

- Will the data be used as the basis for certain policy decisions or the creation of new ordinances, regulations, rules, etc.?

- Will the data be used to assess or evaluate a certain local government department or service or product?

- Will the statistics or data be used as the basis for making certain budgetary or financial decisions?

- Will the data be used to assess or evaluate the performance of certain local government managers or employees?

- In all of these situations, check to see if the statistics or data align with how they were intended to be used in the first place.

- Check whether the government officials, managers or employees are *interpreting* or *applying* the statistics or data in ways that are logical and valid, or are they extrapolating too much, or generalizing too much?

The bottom line is that statistics, data and numbers are only valid and useful if they are being used in the proper and valid *context.* If not, then the local government officials, managers and/or employees need to provide answers as to why not.

Chapter 2:
A Toolbox for Dealing Successfully with Local Government

1. **Case Study:** Case studies involve a particular method of research. Rather than using large samples and following a rigid protocol to examine a limited number of variables, case study methods involve an in-depth, longitudinal examination of a single example. They provide a systematic way of looking at events, collecting data, analyzing information, and reporting the results. As a result, the researcher may gain a sharpened understanding of why the incident happened as it did, and what might become important to study more extensively in future research.

   The case studies used in this book are not intended to be formal, in-depth research processes. They are simply illustrations or anecdotal descriptions of some typical situations that people often encounter in dealing with local government.

2.   **Dialogue:** A dialogue is a conversation between two or more people. In our usage, dialogue seeks to engage the participants in deeply understanding a particular problem or issue and in developing a consensus around the ideal solution. A dialogue is an open, inclusive, professional, low-key conversation that is focused on the development of mutual understandings and agreement, as ways to identify "points of energy" where everyone in the dialogue agrees on a particular idea and is strongly committed to implementing that solution over several months or years. The dialogue process is also focused on building consensus for future efforts and moving forward.

In the world of politics and government, however, the preferred modes of verbal communication are speeches or lectures (one-way communication for some period of time, while everyone else is passively listening), or debates (where two or more people are taking different positions or advocating particular policy, etc.).

In this type of speech or debate, the focus is on winning. One side takes a particular position on some issue and wins out over the others. These kinds of discussions tend to be *exclusive* rather than inclusive, and they also tend to be *closed* rather than open.

We prefer *dialogue* as the best verbal communication and decision-making process, because through *dialogue* we take the time to identify and understand the issues involved, and to explore all of the potential "solution sets." And, in dialogue, there is continuous effort to build agreement (a point of energy) which will support sustained work to implement the preferred solution.

Speeches, lectures, debates and discussion usually lead to decision-making that is driven by voting, or by top-down directives. When this happens, those who lose the vote are no longer committed to implementing the solution advocated by the winner. And when officials or managers issue top-down directives, there are often misunderstandings and resistance from those who are on the receiving end. This can also lead to grudges, silent acquiescence or, in some cases, outright rebellion or sabotage.

3.   **Examining unexamined assumptions:** When citizens or groups are working on an issue or one of its components, one area that can create significant problems is *making assumptions.* For example, if the purpose of a local citizens' group is to reduce the crime rate in their neighborhood, town or city, we generally *assume* that such a purpose is valid, legitimate and desirable.

But is it?

Effective Action Teams need to take the time to examine any assumptions that are critical to the success of any given project in working with local government. The clear guideline here is *never assume anything and ALWAYS examine unexamined assumptions on the front end of developing your project implementation plan.* Take the time and energy to check out each critical assumption, to make sure that it is valid, accurate, appropriate and desirable. Leave nothing to chance.

By *examining our assumptions,* we often discover new insights and ideas about the problem, and learn better ways to solve it. Also, we can avoid unforeseen obstacles from holding up the project. As colleague Don Prentice puts it: "It is not what you think of that causes a project to fail, it is what you *don't* think of."

4.   **Collaborating:** Solving problems or issues with local government is not easy. It takes time, energy, expertise, solid information, funding, and hard work. One secret to success in all of this is to seek out ways to work with those involved in ways that are *collaborative* and *cooperative* rather than *competitive.* The idea here is to identify and implement the ideal solution or set of solutions for a given problem or issue so that everybody wins.

Also, by working in a collaborative mode, citizens' groups can work with local government officials, managers and/or employees to *co-create* new and better solution sets. As the saying goes, "two heads are better than one." When local citizens' groups "put their heads together" with local government officials, managers or employees, then everyone is moving in the same direction and the chances of implementing the ideal solution are greatly increased. The implementation process has a much better chance of being *sustained* over time---for months or years, rather than days or weeks.

Working collaboratively is not always possible, but when it is, people should take the time and devote the energy and funding to do so. The payoff is better solutions that are sustained and supported for many years.

Beating the competition often sounds good, but when local citizens' groups *win* on a given issue or problem by *defeating* local government, what usually happens is that the officials, managers and employees will do what they are supposed to do because they have lost a particular battle, but they won't like it. They will figure out ways to slow it down or make it fail, if they can. Then everybody loses.

5. **Connections:** The term "connections" is vernacular for having personal and/or professional working relationships with certain individuals who hold positions of power in any given organization. Citizens and groups need to initiate, build and continuously improve their personal and professional "connections" with the officials, managers and employees in local government. Building and maintaining these "connections" take time and persistence but, over the long haul, these relationships pay big dividends.

Chapter 3:
The Invisible Government:
Special Districts and Special Interests

There are no additional special terms or jargon in the glossary for Chapter 3. All of the specific local government terms or jargon have been defined within the chapter itself.

Chapter 4:
A Unique Form of Special Districts:
School Districts

1. **Governance of school districts:** Most of the time, we tend to think of our public school districts and public schools as educational institutions. We need to remember, however, that they are also political institutions, and as such they have certain systems, processes and working relationships which determine how they are *governed*. The definition of the term *governance,* when referring to public school districts and schools, refers to how decisions are made about the policies, procedures and rules for the operation of our local school districts and schools, and how those policies, procedures and rules will be implemented.

Chapter 5:
Local Court Systems

There are no additional special terms or jargon in the glossary for Chapter 5. All of the specific local government terms or jargon have been defined within the chapter itself.

Chapter 6:
Putting It All Together:
Leverage and Persuasion

There are no additional special terms or jargon in the glossary for Chapter 6. All of the specific local government terms or jargon have been defined within the chapter itself.

Endnotes
Introduction

1. Most high school, college and university courses on government, civics or political science tend to spend relatively little time on local government. Frequently, emphasis is placed on the fundamentals of the U.S. Constitution, landmark U.S. Supreme Court decisions, the structure and functions of the federal government and those of the state governments. Also, the scant information in these courses about local government is limited to descriptions of the different forms and types, with limited information on how local governments really function.

2. Some typical examples of citizen complaints about dealing with local government bureaucracies include: Property taxes are too high; police or fire services are too slow, are inconsistent, or too costly; garbage collection is inconsistent, poorly done or too costly; local streets and roads are poorly maintained; there is too much housing development (sprawl) or not enough housing development; there is too much crime and violence; local government officials are incompetent or corrupt; the services provided by local government are of low quality or are too costly.

3. All layers of local government, regardless of their names (county, parish, borough, city, municipality, special district, local courts, etc.), are *organizational systems.* This means that they all have *organizational structures* (typically an executive function like a city manager or mayor or county manager), *organizational processes* (typically a legislative function that enacts ordinances or policies or bureaucratic procedures, rules, regulations, etc.) and *organizational working relationships* (typically administrative functions by people

who work in the various departments, commissions, districts or agencies; all of these people operate and work together in an *organizational culture*--the power arrangements, common values, beliefs, patterns of behavior, language, etc.).

4. The term *leverage points* was first introduced to us by our colleague Don Prentice, an expert in systems design and analysis who spent the first half of his career as a computer systems designer for such companies as IBM, NCR, RCA, etc. Don then started his own consulting career where he specialized in helping businesses to improve their organizational structures, processes and working relationships. Along the way he did an in-depth analysis of the problems that were common to most businesses and discovered that they all lacked adequate capacity for effective organizational growth and improvement. He also discovered that in all organizations there are critical interface points in the organizational structures and processes that must be identified in order to implement effective organizational growth and change. He called these interface points *leverage points* because changes implemented at these points create a chain reaction of changes in the rest of the organization.

5. *Idealism or cynicism simply does not work*: We wrote this to address two of the key fallacies that people encounter when they try to work with local government. Some believe that as the "owners" of local government (they elect the government officials and pay taxes that fund it), they have the power to tell local government officials what to do and when to do it. In *theory,* the power and authority possessed by local officials does come from the people, but that does not mean that they can order officials around. Other people have essentially given up on local government, perhaps seeing it as a corrupt cesspool of greedy officials who steal from the people, and it will never change. This view of local government is also wrong, and it is a poor justification for citizens to ignore local government.

6. The term "bureaucracy" has become a dirty word in our present political dialogue, and "bureaucrats" are often depicted as lazy, unresponsive, greedy, self-centered, incompetent "government workers" who spend most of their days getting paid for doing little or nothing. This view is inaccurate, incomplete and just

plain wrong. Moreover, this flawed view of bureaucracies and bureaucrats *severely limits* the effectiveness of local people in dealing with any layer of local government. Bureaucracies are simply the organizational structures and processes that are necessary to implement the day-to-day operations of any layer of local government, and bureaucrats are the people who work in them. Like all organizations, bureaucracies vary in their efficiency and effectiveness, but they are made up of people who work within the limits of prescribed laws, ordinances, regulations, policies and rules. Over time, all bureaucracies develop their own organizational culture. The key is to understand the most effective way to work with the people in this culture, no matter the department

7. *Administrative Law is defined as "the body of law governing administrative agencies". It is broken down to include administrative rules, regulations and procedures for government agencies and bodies; the scope of agency authority, in particular individual privacy; and enforcement powers of agencies.* This formal definition is quoted on the website of Coover and Barr, Attorneys at Law: http://www.cooverbarr.com/faqs.html#administrative.   In simpler terms, administrative law consists of the rules, regulations and procedures developed by local government departments, agencies, commissions, etc. to carry out federal laws, state laws, and local ordinances or policies. Administrative law is *delegated law* because the authority of those who work in local government bureaucracies is given to them by those in higher positions of power: county, borough or parish supervisors, city council members, special district boards or commissions, local court judges, etc.

8. The definition of *political power* has been researched and discussed in a number of history and political science books. For those who would like to delve into the whole subject of *political power* we recommend the following:

    McDonald, Forrest – *Alexander Hamilton, A Biography*, W.W. Norton and Company, N.Y. 1982

Goodwin, Doris Kearns – *Team of Rivals – The Political Genius of Abraham Lincoln* – Simon and Schuster, N.Y., 2006

Smith, Jean Edward – *FDR,* Random House, N.Y. 2007

Kennan, George F. – *Around the Cragged Hill*, Norton and Company, N.Y. 1993

Morris, Edmund – *Theodore Rex*, Modern Library-Random House, N.Y. 2001

Chapter 1: Pragmatism
A Strategy for Dealing Effectively with Local Government

1. For more in depth information on local government *charters* please see the National League of Cities website: http://www.nlc.org/about_cities/cities_101/153.aspx.

    Our democratic form of government, as embodied in the U.S. Constitution, does indeed derive its power and its legitimacy from the people but it is not a "pure" democracy, where the citizens participate directly in making governance decisions. At the local level, we do have a few places in the United States where local citizens participate directly in "town hall meetings" and they do discuss and vote on local government policies and operations, but these forms of "direct democracy" are very few in number and they exist mainly in the New England states. The federal government, the governments of the fifty states, and 99% of all local governments in the United States, are "representative democracies."

2. A cynical view of the term **statistics** was popularized in the United States by Mark Twain (among others), who attributed it to the 19th-century British Prime Minister Benjamin Disraeli (1804–1881): "There are three kinds of lies: lies, damned lies, and statistics." However, the phrase is not found in any of Disraeli's works and the earliest known appearances were years after his death. Other coiners have therefore been proposed. The most plausible, given current evidence, is Englishman Sir

Charles Wentworth Dilke (1843–1911). Please see the Wikipedia website:
http://en.wikipedia.org/wiki/Lies,_damned_lies,_and_statistics.
http://www.twainquotes.com/Statistics.html
http://www.york.ac.uk/depts/maths/histstat/lies.htm

Chapter 2:
A Toolbox for Dealing Successfully with Local Government

1.   The quote about "getting the right people on the bus" comes from a book by Jim Collins entitled *Good to Great – Why some companies make the leap and others don't,* HarperCollins Publishers, Inc., 10 East 53rd Street, New York, New York, 2001, pages 41, 56, and 58. We used the phrase "getting the right people on the right bus" in the context of forming local citizens groups and the "right bus" refers to an *Effective Action Team (EAT)* rather than the typical committee.

2.   "A true champion remains calm in situations that unnerve ordinary people." Stated by Homer D. "Buzz" Ostrom, circa 1955.

3.   The *Conditions for Change*™ tool was created and developed by our good friend and colleague Don Prentice. Don Prentice is an expert in *Applied Systems Thinking (AST)* and he first developed the *Conditions for Change*™ when he was working as a systems designer for some of the leading-edge companies in computer design and computer network design: IBM, RCA, NCR, etc. Don realized that implementing new ways of designing things and new ways of managing complex business projects involved *change* and he studied the extensive literature on "change" and "change processes" and then developed this simple, practical, powerful "tool."

4.   The "Fish Bone Diagram" was developed by Kaoru Ishikawa in the 1960s, who pioneered quality management processes in the Kawasaki shipyards, and in the process became one of the founding fathers of modern management.

It was first used in the 1960s, and is considered one of the seven basic tools of quality control. It is known as a fishbone diagram because of its shape, similar to the side view of a fish skeleton. Please see the Wikipedia website: http://en.wikipedia.org/wiki/Ishikawa_diagram

http://www.vectorstudy.com/management_gurus/kaoru_ishikawa.htm

5.   There are many different kinds of *Project Implementation Plans* and the one we use in this book is a very simplified version. For some solid examples of useful tools and methods in project planning and implementation go to the *Free Management Library*™ at: http://managementhelp.org/plan_dec/project/project.htm. Authenticity Consulting, LLC, provides the Library as a **free community resource**. The Library has its own logo and domain name, apart from Authenticity Consulting, LLC. Carter McNamara, of Authenticity Consulting, LLC, began putting resources on the Internet for others, back in the very early 1990s when he had the privilege of working with the "Gopher" tool at the University of Minnesota. (The University's tool was one of the first user-friendly tools for uploading, downloading and managing files on the Internet.) Also, please see: http://www.information-management-architect.com/project-implementation-plan.html

6.   The *Transformation Map*™ was also created and developed by our friend and colleague Don Prentice. Don worked on many complex business projects for some leading-edge companies and later he also worked on similar projects as a business consultant. He discovered that when these complex projects failed or did not produce the full range of desired outcomes it was because there was no adequate plan in place to guide the whole transformation process. He also discovered that many managers did not take the time to adequately define and describe the *desired outcomes* for a given project, or to make sure that the *necessary and sufficient conditions* were in place to deliver the *desired outcomes*. He also found that many managers operated on the basis of using lots of *unexamined assumptions* about the

current conditions that were or were not in place in their companies when they were about to launch a new project and they underestimated what it would take to change those *current conditions.* The result of Don's work was another practical, powerful "tool" – the *Transformation Map™.*

7.   This critical notion was also developed by Don Prentice. He realized that by using his *Transformation Map™* he could avoid the trap of failing to identify all of the critical issues, components and conditions that were required for the success of a given project.

Chapter 3:
The Invisible Government:
Special Districts and Special Interests

1.   *Special Districts* is the term or descriptor generally used to describe a wide range of local government entities that usually provide specific services to local or regional residents in a given city or county (parish). As we indicate in Chapter 3 there are many different names that are used to describe *special districts,* and they vary by state and region. In almost every state, there are *special district associations* which provide information and training for local citizens to serve on boards and commissions that govern special districts, and these *special district associations* also engage in lobbying and consulting with the federal, state, and local governments. Some examples of these *special district associations* may be found at:

The California Special Districts Association:
http://www.csda.net/

The Special Districts Association of Oregon:
http://www.sdao.com/

The Florida Association of Special Districts:
http://www.fasd.com/

The Utah Association of Special Districts:
http://www.uasd.org/index.php?option=com_frontpage&Item
id=57

The South Carolina Association of Special Purpose Districts:

http://www.scspd.com/

The Ohio Public Transit Association:
http://www.ohiopublictransit.org/04links.html

2.   *Special Districts* or, as they are also known in many states, *Special Purpose Districts,* have existed in the United States since the early 1800's. For a good description of Special Districts or Special Purpose Districts please go to the following research report prepared by the state of Washington: http://www.mrsc.org/publications/spd.pdf

3.   In legal terms, special districts are "agents" or "agencies" whose legal power and authority comes from the state governments. For a detailed legal description of special districts please go to *The Free Dictionary by Farlex* at http://encyclopedia.thefreedictionary.com/Special-purpose+district.

4.   Please see http://www.mwdh2o.com/.

5.   Please see http://www.rtachicago.com/.

6.   For a more detailed description of the creation of special districts please see: *What's So Special About Special Districts?* - at the following website: http://www.rsrpd.org/public/Whatsso.pdf, and the New York and New Jersey Port Authority website: http://www.panynj.gov/corporate-information/governance.html.

7.   *Local Agency Formation Commissions* or LAFCOs are a unique form of local government in California. For detailed information on LAFCOs, please go to: http://www.calafco.org/about.htm.

8.   Please see:
http://www.sos.georgia.gov/Archives/how_may_we_help_yo
u/county_line_disputes/County%20Line%20Disputes%20Pro
cess%20Summary_vrr%20final.pdf.

9.   Please see:
      http://www.mrsc.org/subjects/governance/spd/spdmain.aspx.

10.   Please see: http://www.la-
      par.org/Publications/PDF/Textchap6.pdf.

11.   Please see: http://law.justia.com/iowa/codes/2009/title-
      9/subtitle-2/.

12.   Please see: http://www.cvmvcd.org/specialdistrict.htm.

13.   Please see:
      http://taxdollars.ocregister.com/2010/11/18/special-districts-
      have-nest-eggs-worth-billions/68538/.

Chapter 4:
A Unique Form of Special Districts:
School Districts

1.   Please see: http://www.pbs.org/onlyateacher/horace.html
      http://en.wikipedia.org/wiki/Horace_Mann.

2.   Please see:
      http://nces.ed.gov/programs/projections/projections2018/sec6
      b.asp.

3.   Please see: http://nces.ed.gov/fastfacts/display.asp?id=77.

Chapter 5:
Local Court Systems

1.   Please see:
      http://www.ncsconline.org/D_Research/Ct_Struct/.

2.   Please see:
      http://www.ncsconline.org/D_Research/Ct_Struct/.

3.   All of the key legal terms and definitions are documented in
      the *Summary of American Law* by Martin Weinstein,
      published by The Lawyers Co-Operative Publishing
      Company, Rochester, New York, 1988.

Chapter 6:
Putting It All Together:
Leverage and Persuasion

1.   Quotes from Dr. Peter Drucker may be found at: http://www.brainyquote.com/quotes/authors/p/peter_drucker_ 3.html.